GO SEE *the*
PRINCIPAL

GO SEE *the* PRINCIPAL

TRUE TALES *from the* School TRENCHES

Gerry Brooks

Da Capo
LIFE
LONG

Da Capo Press
Hachette Book Group
1290 Avenue of the Americas, New York, NY 10104
www.dacapopress.com
@DaCapoPress

Printed in the United States of America

First Edition: July 2019

Published by Da Capo Press, an imprint of Perseus Books, LLC,
a subsidiary of Hachette Book Group, Inc.

The Hachette Speakers Bureau provides a wide range of authors for speaking events. To find out more, go to www.hachettespeakersbureau.com or call (866) 376-6591.

The publisher is not responsible for websites (or their content) that are not owned by the publisher.

Print book editorial production by Lori Hobkirk at the Book Factory. Interior design by Cynthia Young at Sagecraft.

Library of Congress Cataloging-in-Publication Data has been applied for.

ISBNs: 978-0-7382-8506-1 (paperback); 978-0-7382-8507-8 (ebook)

LCCN: 2019931464

LSC-C

10 9 8 7 6 5 4 3 2

With thanks to Claire Zulkey for the writing assistance.

Contents

Introduction

A Note from the Principal's Desk

I'm an educator who has taught every elementary school grade, with the exception of kindergarten.* I've spent six years in the classroom, two years as an intervention specialist, and 12 years as an administrator, plus time as a youth minister. These days, I'm the principal of Liberty Elementary school in Lexington, Kentucky. I'm proud to say that since I arrived in 2014, the school has made great progress as we began to prioritize climate and culture throughout the building. When I came to the school, we were just below the middle of the pack when it came to state testing for our district. With an amazing staff, we quickly moved up the ranks into a proficient rating within one year.

We've steadily improved each year, gaining more knowledge of what our students need to grow both academically and emotionally. While I believe I helped set the stage for improvement, I do not in any way take credit for the high achievement at Liberty. That's all due to the hard work of a dedicated staff.

---

*Because I'm not insane. I love that kindergarteners all want to be your best friend, but the "um, um, um, um" that permeates their conversations is just one straw too many for me.

I believe creating a culture of respect, support, and encouragement helps our staff focus on what's more important: the students. When this happens, everything else falls into place.

Education was a natural career path for me. Growing up in Rockledge, Florida, I was an outgoing kid. I valued attention, having lots of friends, and involvement in school activities. When it came to summer jobs, I preferred to babysit, teach swim lessons, or work as a camp counselor rather than, say, bag groceries at Kroger. I enjoyed spending time with kids and thrived under the responsibilities and opportunities for leadership that come with those jobs. As an undergraduate at Troy University in Alabama figuring out what to do with my life, it was an easy decision to pursue a career in education. Unlike my father, a school coach who resented having to spend time as a teacher, I truly enjoyed my work.

However, teaching can be stressful, even when you love it. After a fantastic first year at Liberty, I noticed that the mood of the school and teachers changed radically in the spring of 2015. I couldn't for the life of me figure out what happened until I began to listen to conversations about an upcoming state assessment.

By far, the most stressful aspect of education is the pressure we feel from assessments—note the "s" on that word! Nonstop assessments are a regular part of education today. Teachers often have to sacrifice up to six weeks of daily instruction to cram required assessments into their school days. Confident, skilled teachers at Liberty were now in "What if I didn't do enough?" mode, wondering (more like panicking) about how their students would perform. The staff was stressed in a way I hadn't seen before.

I couldn't figure out how to help. One day, as usual, I got to school at 5:00 a.m. because . . . well, basically because no one is there to bother me that early. In those days, I walked the building every morning for 30 minutes to get some much-needed exercise. As I paced through the halls that late April, I walked by blank walls and empty bulletin boards with no student work on them. That reminded me of how ridiculous our state assessment system had become—the state of Kentucky requires us to put away all instructional materials from our classrooms before state assessments, including things posted in the hallways, because, you know, we wouldn't want a student to go to the bathroom during an assessment and suddenly learn how to add fractions because of a hallway display that might accidentally help him do better on the state assessment!

I decided a way to break the stress would be to create a short video for the staff where I'd pretend to call out the art teacher's bulletin board in the hallway because she had left some staples in the corkboard. I stood in front of her bulletin board, which was completely blank aside from some purple background paper, a green border, and some offending staples, and lectured:

I know you aren't used to this because you are an art teacher and all . . . but here at Liberty we don't help students on state testing by leaving things on the walls. I have noticed you left some staples up, and when students see staples, they are going to begin to think, "I went to Staples to get a computer and there weren't many there, so I had to push my way through the day so that's an example of scarcity." So, these staples need to come down.

I wanted to remind our staff how dumb the situation had become. I hoped the half-minute video would relieve the stress of testing and lighten the mood of a fantastic staff that had doubted how much they had accomplished in the previous eight months.

While videos like these were originally made to communicate with Liberty teachers, to my surprise, they began to go viral—the most popular, where I asked for the community's support during teacher strikes, drew in more than 10.7 million viewers. I have a slight Southern accent in real life (or so non-Southern people tell me), but in the videos I took it to the next level, incorporating the speaking styles of the Alabamans I met at Troy and several kids in our school who speak that exact way (so, no, I don't actually call myself the "purnciple" when I'm home.)

Since I posted my first video, what started as a way to entertain my friends, family, and staff members has grown into a second career, as I've been invited to speak at a number of educational conferences and engagements around the country to commiserate with and motivate other educators.

I think the videos connect with people—teachers especially—not only because I use a funny accent but because behind each humorous topic is something real that affects educators. For instance, I made a video about teacher bathroom etiquette after the alarming experience of walking in on a substitute teacher on the toilet because she had neglected to lock the bathroom door.

Bathrooms are funny; that's why there's a whole genre of humor devoted to them. But when I show that film at educational conferences, I use it to illustrate the larger point of why it's important for a school's staff to get on the same page.

The stakes of our jobs are high, which is why I feel strongly that administrators, teachers, staff, and parents can more effectively create a positive atmosphere at school.

Kids rely on school staff in ways you wouldn't even think of. We have a teacher at Liberty who matches everything she wears to her clothes: her shoes, her watch, her jewelry. Sometimes in the hallway she'll run into a girl who dresses the same way. They've built a relationship even though they're not in the same class. It may seem like a small thing, but that connection strengthens that young girl's confidence, security, and attitude toward learning.

STAFF BATHROOM ETIQUETTE RULES

✓ There is a lock on the door for a reason. Make sure you click the bathroom lock. If you don't hear click, it's not locked. It's very traumatizing to walk in on a staff member in the bathroom.

✓ When the toilet paper is gone, call the custodian. Don't just leave and not tell anyone because the next person that comes in doesn't realize there's no toilet paper and it causes . . . some stress.

✓ If you share a bathroom, and you have fluffied up that bathroom with lace and flowers and generic Longaberger baskets, put something manly in there so the men will feel welcome. Like a bobble head or a superhero poster.

✓ If you happen to have bathrooms where there's one for men's and one for women's, don't yell at the men when there is a line at the women's bathroom. That is not our fault. And stop trying to sneak into the men's bathroom. If we snuck into the lady's bathroom you would say "Gross." So stop sneaking into the men's bathroom. Gross.

✓ Most important, air freshener don't make the air fresher. Stop spraying 42 seconds worth of air freshener. It's just making things worse.

✓ If you have taco Tuesday at your house, Wednesday might be a good day for you get a doctor's appointment, so you could be off school and bless everyone.

We make a difference in kids' lives—and the lives of their parents—that we can see daily. When you're negative, the kids are negative, and when you're happy and work well together, the children and parents feed off that energy. These kids are all future adults in our community. What kind of people do we want to send out in the world? Positive people who work out their problems, or negative, angry young adults? What we model for them makes a big difference.

Administrators, teachers, and parents don't always have to agree, but they need to reach an understanding through communication, compassion, and compromise.

It's pretty simple.

When you **communicate**, school teams talk through every decision and everybody gets a say. Imagine five teachers trying to plan a Valentine's Day party and four of them want to have cake, show a movie, and do a craft where all the kids decorate a box, but the fifth teacher says, "That's not what I want to do in my classroom." Instead of the other teachers steamrolling her, or that teacher getting passive-aggressive about it, the group needs to clarify, "This is exactly what I think. What do you all think? Why do we think this?"

When we have **compassion** toward one another, we consider the reasons for people's opinions. Why doesn't that teacher want to do the same party? Can she not afford the time? Will she not be able to get the same parent support other teachers get? Does she think it's going be chaotic and overwhelming? We have to remember that there are valid reasons for people's opinions.

When we **compromise**, we see a positive result. I think too often people forget that it's okay to walk away disagreeing, as long as they've communicated and exercised compassion first. If the end result is, "My party will look like this and your party will look like that," as long as everybody understands that, we're good.

But even schools with great atmospheres have bad days—when lesson plans fall through, when parents call us irate because they don't like the way something was handled at recess, when kids throw tantrums because they have to use the same spoon for their applesauce *and* mashed potatoes, and of course, assessments—when we need humor to get us through the week.

At my teacher events, I like to show the videos to get everyone laughing, and then I talk more seriously about how important it is to get everyone—parents, teachers, and administrators—on the same page. I hope to do the same here in this book—use humor to share what I've learned during my time in education and what I've learned from other educators—so we can all literally be on the same page.

There are many opportunities for improvement in a child's educational life, so in this book I try to address each of them and call out how administrators can better support teachers, teachers can better communicate with parents, and parents can better understand their child's teacher—all in the spirit of serving students.

My goal is to empower educators in order to empower all of us. I'm here to motivate and advocate, and I hope to inspire not just other teachers and administrators, but anyone who's ever known a teacher—who has ever been positively impacted by a teacher—to do the same.

Suriously.

PART 1

BEFORE THE BELL RINGS

Setting Up Teachers,
Parents, and Administrators
for a Great Year

1

"BUT I DON'T WANT TO GO BACK TO SCHOOL!"

Principal Tips for Motivating and Bonding Your Team

The first day of school is always a momentous occasion for parents and kids. Teachers also get swept up the excitement—even though their first day occurs a few days earlier—without many "first day of school" photos and hardly any tears.

I think opening day for teachers should be as fun and exciting as humanly possible. It's the first time your whole staff gathers together, which presents a tremendous opportunity to bolster personal relationships.

You don't need to rent an escape room or order an expensive catered breakfast for a strong start to the year (although nobody would mind donuts and coffee). I've heard teachers complain, "We don't want to spend three hours on games when we could be getting our classrooms ready," so simplicity is key.

Principals, I've developed some simple icebreakers that you can try at your school. I like to spread these out throughout the meetings so there are little breaks for fellowship in between moments of actual work.

If you don't have much time to prepare, an easy activity is to give the teachers little packages that contain items like a fun-sized pack of M&Ms or Starburst. I like to use cans of Vienna sausages because it's funny and there are seven hot dogs per can, but your staff may prefer candy to processed meat. I ask everyone to open theirs and share one fact about themselves to go with each item. It also helps to put up a PowerPoint slide with prompts like "What did you do this summer?" "Where did you grow up?" "Do you have children?" "What's your favorite movie?" That way people who might be shy or who blank when all eyes are on them will have something to say. With this activity, teachers who might not know each other are more likely to have topics to bond over while they're on recess duty or bump into each other in the parking lot. They can say, "My mother is from California" or "I was at that concert this summer too!"

If you have a bit more time, try a "Blast from the Past" PowerPoint. A few days before opening day, I go on Facebook and find meaningful photos of as many teachers as I can from earlier in their lives, like wedding or graduation photos. I play the slide show and ask each teacher to tell us something about the day their photo was taken. Then I ask, "What's one way you've changed or grown since then?" This leads into a good discussion of how they can grow this year as teachers and how they want their students to grow as well.

If you have time to research and already have established a good relationship with much of your staff, pull social media pictures your teachers have posted of themselves with their children, and ask each staff member to share something special about their child. I'll play a game where I ask the teachers to guess whose child is in the photo. "What aspirations do you have for your child?" I then ask, which leads to a discussion about how all parents have certain dreams for their kids—kids like the ones we're in charge of seven hours per day. I emphasize that it's our job to help those children reach their parents' goals and aspirations. It sends a powerful message to see other teachers as parents and to remember that each parent at home wants something great for his or her child.

If you're blessed with more time or have an active parent-teacher association (PTA), there's the baggage icebreaker. I've spent a few days over the summer gathering used suitcases from Goodwill and the Salvation Army, which usually cost $2 or $3 each. If you're on a budget, you can email a few dozen parents and ask them to lend the school two pieces of luggage and drop them off a few days before opening day. Then, the night before our first meeting, I put a suitcase in everyone's room. I send my staff a text message that says, "When you come to the meeting, bring the baggage that was left in your classroom," and instruct them to leave the bags in the hall. You end up with a huge pile of luggage, which can lead into a discussion about how we can have a more positive year by leaving behind old emotional baggage we've carried around, whether it's anxiety about seeing parents who stressed us out last year, issues with the lesson plan, or overwhelming problems with disorganization. I put out a big sign that reads, "Baggage We've Left Behind," and leave it there for a few days before school starts. Contemplating a fresh start is a release for everyone, and it's a great visual when the teachers see 50 pieces of luggage piled up outside the staff meeting area. This is an especially effective activity if you're at a new school or there's been a lot of flux.

If you can get your staff bonded and optimistic ahead of time, this sets the right tone not just for the first day but for the whole year, and the benefits trickle down to the kids and their parents. Plus, you might just get some extra hot dogs for your lunch.

2

CLASSROOM PLACEMENT
The Methods to Our Madness

At my school, we mail our placement announcements out in July—the letters that tell parents which classrooms their kids are assigned to for the fall. Due to confidentiality, we don't mail the whole list, just a letter that reads, "This is who your child's teacher is gonna be."

Yet somehow the parents figure out which child is in which class, and every year I get at least one silly call from a parent who complains, "I don't want my child with Mrs. Smith."

"Why?"

"Well, I've heard she's a yeller."

I'll ask, "Who have you heard that from?"

"Well, my son walks by her room and says she *looks* like a yeller."

Or, we'll hear this:

"I want Mrs. Smith."

"Why do you want Mrs. Smith?"

"My daughter likes the way she dresses."

Or this:

"I don't want my child with Susie."

"Why not?"

"Susie's mean."

"Okay, we can move your child to another classroom."

"Well, my child has friends in her classroom. Can you move Susie?"

Here's the thing, and I can't reiterate this enough: All parents want what's best for their child. But these parents in particular, who want to control every situation, think they know a teacher's personality, or whether their child can handle a year in a classroom with a particular child. They're not considering the professionalism of the teachers and what they see every day.

It was with this in mind that I made a video in which I discussed the secret codes teachers use on student placement cards as we decide which child goes in which classroom. These cards include spaces for students' names, academic levels, who they should be with and maybe shouldn't be with, along with the most important information of all: codes to describe the children's parents:

SS: The Starbucks Shopper parent who's going to bring you coffee. You want to get that parent.

RRNSU: This stands for Reschedule, Reschedule, Never Shows Up—that parent who doesn't ever show up for conferences but is always trying to reschedule them.

RCP: This is Reality Check Parent, the one who needs little reminders like "No, your child's not gifted. He ain't no prodigy."

HOE: Hatin' On Exes—those parents who are divorced and don't like each other anymore. You gotta make like six copies of everything 'cause they can't share. Good Lord, you had a kid together. Can't you share a newsletter?

GGG: The Good Gift Giver. That's always important to know.

IABYF: It Always Be Your Fault. These parents are always going to blame you for everything.

HSB: This is the Healthy Snack Bringer. Nobody wants a healthy snack bringer as your room parent. Don't be bringin' no carrots to a birthday party. I'm serious.

CGA: Constantly Giving Attitude. You know that parent: "Why I got to bring in some coffee filters as a school supply?" Because I said so. Boom.

WTLC: That's the Way-Too-Late "Conference-r." Those are the parents that always want to have a conference after report cards. "Can I do anything for my child's grades?" Yeah, come in before school report cards come out.

Seriously, parents, the next time you pick up the phone to complain about your child's classroom assignment, remember that the teachers had to carefully juggle the following considerations to create a harmonious classroom that's optimal for learning:

Personalities of students. Teachers often see conflicts between students that aren't big enough to bring to a parent's attention but can cause concern for placing those students in the same class. Are there three or four girls who are bossy and like to be in charge? Then we want to make sure they're not all in the same classroom because then we end up with behavior conflicts among friends. We also look for the shy, quiet students and make sure they've got somebody in the classroom they're comfortable with.

Academic levels. Teachers seriously consider academic levels when creating a class roster. If there's a good balance of high, medium, and low students in a classroom, everybody benefits during class discussions. The high students can bring up a lot of prior knowledge and higher-order questioning. The lower students are able to give input and succeed when they're asked appropriate questions.

Involved parents. This was what inspired the video about the parent codes on student placement cards. Whose parents can send some food in for a party or go along on a field trip? While we may do a good job of splitting up academics and personalities, we might have all the parents that are willing to help out in one classroom, when another classroom doesn't have snacks at a party because nobody was there to help. So, we strive to ensure all teachers have parental support for their class.

Teacher consideration. Administrators need to make sure all teachers are present when they finalize classroom placement. There's a lot to be said for a teacher who says, "I really struggled with that child's parent," "I know that girl well because she lives in my neighborhood, and I don't want her in my classroom," or "I know that family well and I *do* want her in my classroom." Make sure you consult your specials-area teams, the librarian who goes, "When they're with me, these girls fight all the time," or the physical education (PE) teacher who says, "These two kids are very competitive." A lot of times, you'll separate a kid from a distracting friend in second grade, and then by third grade they're put back together because the first grade teachers weren't part of the conversation and no one can remember why those two were separated to begin with, and now they're back together, more distracting than ever.

And that's almost as bad as carrots at a classroom birthday party.

3

SCHOOL SUPPLIES
Yes, We Really Need All That Stuff

Several years ago, Staples released a funny commercial in which a father danced around the store to the song "It's the Most Wonderful Time of the Year," tossing school supplies in his shopping cart while his children watched, stone-faced.

I wish all parents were that excited about pencils, folders, and protractors, but some push back when supply lists are sent home. They grumble when they have to spend $25, $50, or $100 on supplies, but they don't understand that if the student doesn't bring that stuff in, then it lands in the school's lap—or even the teacher's personal wallet—to supply them.

Parents need to follow a school supply list and not buy things their students just want. I remember as a kid pushing back against the school's "No Trapper Keeper" rule. We'd say, "But they look so cool, and they're well-organized!" but the fact was, they didn't fit in the school desks. School supply lists aren't made arbitrarily—if certain colored folders or coffee filters are on the list, it's because the teacher needs them for a specific reason. (For the record, coffee filters are a great, inexpensive alternative to paper plates for snack time.) Parents should remember that a lot of time goes into creating a supply list and teachers don't just ask for things willy-nilly. Your teacher didn't ask for Crayola markers just to make your life hard. It's because when you purchase markers from the dollar store, they go dry within a week and a half. If a teacher asks for five red folders, buy five red folders. There's a reason they want those. "My child doesn't like that color" or "I couldn't find that brand" aren't valid excuses to not follow the list.

Schools ask parents to chip in for supplies so that they can spend school funds on other resources. If we have $116 to spend per child, we use it on items like textbooks, computers, smart boards, or *TIME for Kids*—materials that parents don't have access to and things they don't want to spend their money on. Let's say we ask each parent to bring in a package of notebook paper that costs $1. If we don't, my school now has $750 less in its budget to spend on classroom materials.

There's a time/money equation when it comes to school supplies. Some parents are willing to pay more for the convenience of a box program where the supplies are ordered and delivered to the school, no muss, no fuss. If you have a little more time and want to save some money, there's Amazon. And if you're well-organized and patient, a trip to Walmart or Target to shop the aisles is the most cost-efficient approach. I'm personally still in favor of that method, especially if you take your child with you, even if it takes the most time. School shopping is a rite of passage and can be a fun family activity. I still have fond memories of taking my kids shopping in the fall, and how excited they were to go through the list. I mean, how often does a six-year-old get to go shopping? Plus, this can be an educational opportunity to discuss price comparisons and budgets.

If cost is sincerely an issue for a family, there's always a way around it. Churches or family resource centers can step up with donations. If you can't afford supplies, don't build up resentment or grumble to other parents. Go in and say to the teacher, "We can't afford this." Teachers, of all people, understand strict budgets, and are happy to help, especially if the alternative is for them to have to pony up themselves for the supplies.

Another good lesson for parents and kids alike that comes via school supplies is the idea of community property. Teachers often have "community supplies" so that everyone has access to these items and things are equal in class. When you put your child's name on every single marker and the teacher says "Okay, put all your markers in the middle," then your child will get upset if somebody grabs "her" brown marker. Abide by community property rules. Don't put your child's name on all her markers and expect her to be the only one who gets to use them. There are certain things in society we all chip in for—like taxes that pay for libraries, public schools, and road maintenance—and school supplies are a great way to lead into that discussion.

This mentality applies to school activities as well: districts aren't allowed to charge a certain amount for programs and then tell lower-income students that they can't play if they can't pay, so the school budget or fundraising makes them more affordable. So, yes, if you're paying $1,500 for your child's cheerleading program, part of that money may support students who can't otherwise afford to join.

Some parents say, "I don't want to pay for other people's kids," but what kind of example do we set if children whose parents can't afford money for a field trip have to stay behind? How would those children feel, and what message do you send to our own children, to punish those who have less?

Like kids and markers, parents need to think in terms of community property. For those who can afford it, chipping in a little can mean a lot to the parent or teacher who does get hurt when they have to pay for an extra pack of pencils.

So, while you're shopping for school, remember that the goal is to enable your child's teacher so all of his classmates can learn and feel good about themselves, and not an evil plot to ruin your day by sending you to four different stores to find the right glue sticks.

4

AGE-APPROPRIATE BEHAVIOR
Finding Your Perfect Grade

All right, boys and girls, everybody come over and sit on the ABC carpet. Find a letter, okay?

So, your teacher's not feeling well today, and. . . . What are you doing? Why are you standing here? Why are you smelling me? It's cologne. I'm glad you like it. Now go sit down. Don't be smelling people. Sit down.

All right, your teacher's not feeling good. We got a sub coming in. She's late, so I'm going. . . . No, your teacher's not dying. She'll be back tomorrow. So I'm going to do your carpet time to. . . . No, we're not calling her and singing "Soft Kitty."

Okay, I'm going to do your carpet time today. Why are you standing up? Yeah, there's a letter R right there. No, you're not allergic to the letter R. Sit down. Right there.

All right, so Z is our letter, I need a Z word. Who has a Z word? Yes. Zendaya? What's a Zendaya? The Disney Channel? No, I'm not writing her name up here. Okay. Anybody got . . . yes, sir. Zombie? I'm not writing "zombie" up here either. Okay, somebody come up with a good z word. Yes, ma'am. Zinfandel?

Is your mama a teacher? Yeah, I'm not writing that word up here either. Zebra. Okay, zebra. I'm just gonna write the word zebra. Okay, it's Z-E . . .

What are you eating? Where did you? . . . Why? . . . Marsh-mallows? Where'd you get marshmallows? In your pocket. Okay, that's disgusting. It's not snack time. It's eight in the morning, go put those in your backpack. Don't do that again.

What do you got in your hand? A Transformer? Are you al-lowed to bring toys? No. Go put it right back there in that box that says "May." You can get that back in May.

Now we're gonna count pennies. You hold these, sweetie. Okay. You got nine pennies, I'm gonna give you one more penny. How many she's got now? Ten. Good job. Okay. Now, I'm gonna trade her 10 pennies for this dime. The dime is the same thing as the 10 pennies. You trade me the 10 pennies for the dime. What you mean, "No?" They're exactly the same. What do you mean "it's a rip-off"? Don't be telling her it's a rip-off. It's the same thing, okay? I'm gonna give her a dime. She's gonna give me 10 pennies. Why you crying? You just keep the 10 pennies. Okay, sit down right there.

Now, we need a meteorologist. Who's gonna go stick their hand out the window and tell us what the weather's like? Okay, yes sir. Go right there. What's the weather like out there? "Fluffy" is not an answer. The weather can't be fluffy. What's it feel like out there? "Sad"? No. I know you're sad that your teacher's not here, but that's not the way. It's gotta be sunny or rainy, or cloudy or snowing or something like that. What is it? Rainy? It's not raining out there. You see any rain? Come sit down.

Okay, so what special are we going to today? Where do you run? "The park"? No, we're not going to the park for . . . we're going to PE. Okay. We're going to PE for specials . . . you know, this is not working. Everybody go get a book and sit in one of those laundry baskets and just silently read to yourself.

I made that video to illustrate *exactly* what happens in a primary classroom on a daily basis. There is some level of this type of age-appropriate behavior for every level of education. Primary students constantly interrupt you due to their excitement, intermediate students roll their eyes and act disinterested, middle school students try to act tough and cool to fit in, and high school students are more interested in just about anything other than your instruction.

This is called acting your age, and teachers need to learn how to roll with it. How can we get angry with the preschool student who moves tables to sit at the spot with the sunbeam in order to feel its warmth, or the kindergartener who gets up and runs across the cafeteria to hug his big brother? I'm not saying we don't need to correct behaviors and help students understand rules, but sometimes teachers get upset over basic age-appropriate behavior and I think it's a waste of energy.

Third grade is personally my sweet spot. I've taught every elementary grade except kindergarten, and to me, third grade is the point by which children are more self-sufficient, but they're still innocent. They still love their teachers and they also have a sense of humor. They're now reading to learn instead of learning to read, and they're big sponges. They're able to follow rules.

Younger students are needy. They struggle with things that frustrate me, like using the word "sad" as a meteorological term. But past third grade, they lose some of that innocence. They get a bit mouthier, a bit more challenging. Middle schoolers come with more drama, like tearful girls whose boyfriends broke up with them. And high schoolers are leaving or have completely left childhood, although they also have more sophisticated levels of curiosity and maturity.

No matter what grade you teach, you will encounter behavior that, while frustrating, is appropriate in terms of development for that group. You may want to say, "What, did you really think you two were going to get married?" to the middle school girl crying over her breakup, but to her, that's her reality. Teachers, it's your job to know what age-appropriate behavior is, look through it, and know when something that might be frustrating is totally normal for the age.

Something great about teaching is that if you're frustrated with age-appropriate behavior, then there's a lot of other grades you can go to. If you're frustrated with kids who constantly want to socialize and argue about who's going to whose party, and who's dating whom, then middle school may not be the right bubble for you. Drop down to fourth grade. And if you're frustrated that kids can't tie their shoes, move up to fifth grade.*

You also have to learn to accept that age-appropriate behavior doesn't change. Thirteen-year olds now are gonna be exactly the same as 13-year-olds will be in 10 years, so if you don't like that, consider a career change.

Every grade level has its burdens, but they all have something great about them, too. My perspective is that whatever grade you currently teach is the most important grade. It's easy to get caught up thinking, "I want to teach third grade, but they've stuck me in eighth grade biology," but for now, eighth grade biology should be the most important grade level to you.

*Well, maybe sixth or seventh.

5

BUSING

How Parents, Teachers, and Administrators Can Keep Those Wheels Going 'Round

Paraprofessionals have to deal with a lot before school even begins, from early morning reading interventionists to the cafeteria workers who serve breakfast, but at least those staff members have the advantage of getting to handle students' chaos without having to drive a large vehicle at the same time.

In addition to the general stress of maintaining a schedule and driving safely, bus drivers are responsible for children they can't even see, who, believe it or not, don't always sit quietly like little angels. Sometimes kids take their food out of their backpacks and spread it around the back seat like it's a picnic. Sometimes they throw up. And on two separate occasions my bus drivers have noticed a commotion in the back only to discover that a student had gotten on the bus with a small animal in his backpack.*

*A baby chick and a kitten, to be specific.

If you're a bus driver reading this book, I hope you know I understand the importance of your job. You are the first face to represent the school to every child you pick up. A smile and a "Good morning!" go a long way to help a student have a good day.

You may be the only adult to witness a father screaming at a child for forgetting his lunch, or a kid being pulled by a frustrated mother as you drive up. That student who climbs aboard your bus is embarrassed for getting screamed at in front of his friends and his day is already off to a rough start. Bus drivers aren't counselors, but an "Are you okay?" or "You know what? You look great today" can go a long way. If necessary, a note to the school office to say, "I just want to let you know that Bobby got into a huge fight with his mother right before school and was upset" can help a teacher who has no idea why Bobby is so mopey. Watch your students carefully. If a child who always talks is suddenly silent, or a smiling, happy child seems sad, that's the opportunity for you to step in and help the school see that something might be wrong.

Drivers, you are vital to the success of every student because you set the school mood for the day. Please understand the importance of your job beyond just transportation and help us start every day right.

Parents, remember that buses are on schedules. They can't wait three or four minutes for your child without being late for school. Make sure you're on time and don't get angry at the driver if your child misses the bus.

It's important to show appreciation for everybody involved in your child's life, from the bus driver to the gym teacher to the custodian. Once, one of our bus drivers brought a plate of cookies into the school office and marveled over it like it was the most amazing thing ever, just because a parent had thought to remember him and said, "Thanks for keeping my children safe." I know that's a bus driver's job, but between sticking to the schedule, driving safely, and monitoring kids' moods and socialization on the bus, they do more than we give them credit for.

Trying to get 600 students on the correct bus at the end of the day is frustrating chaos, especially when you have students try to sneak onto someone else's bus or get distracted by a conversation with friends, a toy, or a device as they walk out and potentially get on the wrong bus. Schools work hard to develop specific systems to make sure this doesn't happen. At Liberty, we have adults at the bus who check off a manifest at day's end. This works well when you have a parent who calls in to say, "My child didn't get off the bus today." You can quickly look at the manifest and see if the child was checked off as having gotten on the bus; 95 percent of the time the child was on the manifest and got off to go home with a friend because she had better afternoon snacks there.

Some schools, especially in small districts, can rely on bus drivers' memories. I loved teaching in Bourbon County, a small district in Kentucky with only three elementary schools, where the drivers knew every student and all their parents. No one ever got away with anything because the bus driver would just call the child's parents right then and there from the bus.

No matter the system, busing always comes with its own stresses. Teachers, here are a few things I've learned that help enforce the priority of getting kids home safely every day:

Teachers should ask students whether they have any transportation changes. Every. Single. Morning. When teachers forget this, then we have a student who runs to the office at 2:30 p.m. to get a bus change right in the middle of dismissal, at a time when the secretary is distracted by parents stopping by or a kindergartener who asks for help with a broken flip-flop.

If you struggle to remember to ask about transportation changes, here's a simple solution:

Teachers should find a wonderful, sweet, bossy child in the classroom. When you have one of those students who loves to be in charge, you simply say, "Billy, would you remind me every morning to see if anybody has transportation changes?" Make him the transportation captain. You'll never get away with forgetting, because I guarantee the transportation captain will be up as soon as you try to start a lesson without having asked about transportation changes. (I also recommend appointing an attendance captain, for those of you who forget to take attendance daily. You know who you are!)

Administrators need to hold teachers accountable. On my first day at Liberty Elementary, my phone rang at 4:30 p.m., just as I got home, about to take a nap. It was the district spokeswoman. Our district spokeswoman is well-respected and a friend of mine now, but she's also one of those people you never want to get a phone call from, like the district attorney, and here she was calling me on my first day of school. She said, "I don't want to panic you, but we're dealing with a lost child." How stressful is that? School gets out at 2:30 p.m., so a child had been missing for two hours. I certainly did panic. I hopped into my car and called the child's teacher, and we searched for the student. It turned out that he'd just gotten on the wrong bus and off at the wrong bus stop because in the midst of trying to create 350 bus tags, we mistakenly put his morning bus as his afternoon bus. His grandmother was at home waiting for him and called the school when he didn't arrive. When we drove by his house he was on the front porch, getting yelled at by his mother and grandmother. We apologized for our error and were extremely thankful he was safe (and a little relieved that the grandmother was madder with him than with us). I felt bad for the child, but as you can imagine, immensely relieved. I remember that day as an example of why administrators have to constantly push teachers on the importance of transportation details, because I never wanted to get a phone call like that again. We had gotten 724 students home safely that day, but it wasn't enough. We needed to get 725 home safely.

Parents can help by being aware that students talk, fall asleep, socialize, and otherwise don't pay attention on buses. Don't get frustrated with the bus driver or teacher when your child misses his bus stop because he was busy telling his friend about the new Pokémon cartoon he saw last night. It's not that parents shouldn't hold schools accountable for getting their kids home safely, but if your child happens to miss his or her stop, it helps to ask, in a way that indicates you support the busy bus driver, how this might have happened.

PART *2*

CLASS IS IN SESSION
How Administrators and
Parents Can Let Teachers Teach

6

FIRST DAY OF SCHOOL

Lights, Cameras (So Many Cameras), Action!

Teachers of little kids have a lot to deal with on the first day of school—the crying, the reluctance to say "goodbye," and lots and lots of questions to answer—and that's just from the parents. Thank you; I'll be here all night.

Savvy schools come up with clever ways to handle parents who are reluctant to part with their kids, like Liberty's Boo Hoo Breakfast. That tradition helps pull parents away from their kids and lets the parents bond (because some of them may be in one another's lives for years). In addition to providing coffee and food in the library, we also hand out goodie bags stuffed with tissues, gum, and a magnet with school information. We greet the parents and talk a little about the school to reassure them, if need be, that their child is safe and will be loved all day.

We allow parents to walk their children to their classrooms for the first few days of school. This helps both the child and the parent get acclimated and relaxed about coming in and familiar with the expectations at morning arrival. But on day four we set up a Goodbye Kiss Zone. This is the spot where parents have to hug and kiss their children

VOCABULARY SPOTLIGHT: CKM

CKM stands for **Crying Kindergarten Mom**. Teachers encounter them the first day of school, the first week of school, and generally kind of anywhere.

CKMs tend to hide in school janitorial closets, crying, in order to stay near their little ones. If you encounter a CKM, you may show empathy, but never joke.

DO say: "I know how you feel. Things are going to be okay."

DO NOT say: "Well, we only lost two or three kindergartners last year." This only makes them cry more.

You can, however, distract a CKM with a Boo Hoo Breakfast. My PTA, which is the smartest PTA in the entire world, hosts these get-togethers, which gather up all the CKMs in the library so they're not in the child's classroom (plus in the library they realize how loud they're crying, so they stop). Then we hop 'em up on Krispy Kremes. Now, you've got a CKM who's not worried about Zumba; instead, she's shoving Krispy Kremes in her mouth. She goes home and crashes from that sugar high, and she sleeps until 2:30 p.m., and we don't have to worry about her again until pickup time. Thanks to the Boo Hoo Breakfast, we don't have 40 CKMs in the parking lot at noon gnawing on their fingernails and wondering whether their child fell in the toilet or tripped over their shoelaces.

goodbye and release them to the school, which is full of staff members ready to help the students maneuver the hallways.

Every year, we have parents get upset that they can't walk their students to their classrooms. We even had a parent blast us on Facebook, saying it was ridiculous and she couldn't believe we had such a stupid rule, so I called her and told her she was the ridiculous one (just kidding).* When parents get upset about this rule, we gently remind them that it becomes a safety issue when 400 adults are wandering around the building.

The stress parents go through on day one (and two, three, and four) is valid. I understand that this child you've protected and watched over is now suddenly in a classroom with 25 other kids and two teachers, and you're not able to help her if her shoes become untied, she can't find her lunch, or she can't open her Lunchable. My own kids were clingy when they were small—the type who kept one arm wrapped around my wife's or my legs all the time. And I have to admit, we loved it. It was actually more stressful to send them off to high school than it was in elementary school because at least there we knew their teachers and friends. You just suck it up and stress all day long and know deep down everything will be okay. When they come home, you think to yourself, *Gosh, I was stressed about nothing*.

Aside from knowing when to let go, there are other ways for parents to make the first day easier for your child's teacher—and don't you want your child's teacher to have the most uncomplicated day possible?

Keep conversations short, or even better, nonexistent. While the first day is one of excitement and reunion, it's not the day for parents to

---

*Parents, never, ever blast your school or teacher on Facebook. It does nothing other than paint you as a bully parent and totally wrecks your relationship with the school. Just sayin'.

encourage their kids to find their teachers from last year, or a time to have a long conversation with a new teacher. If you've got 25 parents arriving and each has a minute with the teacher, they've burned through a half hour of the morning already.

Make sure to attend your school's open house. It gives both you and your child a chance to learn the lay of the land. Walk through the cafeteria and the gym and let your child play on the school playground, so he will feel like this is *his* school, not a scary new place.

If your school requests that you drop off school supplies before the first day, respect that guideline so you don't make your child's teacher juggle boxes and bags of pencils and paper while also greeting students and dealing with CKMs.

If your child is anxious, rehearse the first day ahead of time. Walk the route and say, "I'm going to kiss you and say 'goodbye' here at the door" to build confidence.

Parents these days who have a difficult time saying "goodbye" to their young kids at school often try to explain that their stress is due to their fears for their child's safety. But they need to understand that parents have felt this way forever. It's not a modern thing. Separation is just hard.

Teachers should remember that the first day can be special for older students as well as the little guys. Even high school students like to hear about their teacher's personal lives, their favorite TV shows, and what their favorite subjects were when they were students. Instead of just diving into the syllabus and class rules, spend some time getting to know your students and let them get to know one another. Give them a survey to fill out if your students are at an age where they might be reluctant to share in public. They might not show excitement the way first graders do, but they still care.

On the first day of school, nervous parents just need to remember that teachers and schools have done this for years and they are professionals. As hard as it is to drop children off, smile, and leave, you need to know that they are in safe hands and those teachers care. They're gonna be okay.

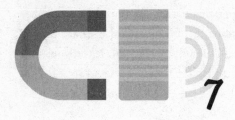

CURRICULUM

Putting the "Can" in "Canned"

Many teachers, especially experienced ones, have a difficult time with what they might call a "canned curriculum"—a curriculum published by an educational company. These curriculums are developed around core content and designed so that teachers can open a book and work their way through it to help their students become successful.

I personally love curriculums like Saxon Math or Go Math because they're research-based tools, especially helpful for new or struggling teachers for whom a road map or script can be a lifesaver.

However, following a published curriculum can come with its own challenges, particularly when states and districts administer assessments out of order with the curriculum. A grade may be tested on comparing and contrasting or denominators in August, but the curriculum doesn't get there until May.

Some schools demand total adherence to the curriculum, which in my opinion takes away from teacher autonomy—experienced teachers know if they need to back up when their students aren't grasping a concept, or when it's time to introduce a fun and educational game that they found on Teachers Pay Teachers that can help students understand fractions.

I think it's ideal to have to have a mixture of both in the classroom. Districts and schools that teach the curriculum to absolute fidelity, with no changes, run the risk of squelching creativity in the classroom. However, I don't think teachers should entirely turn their noses up at published curriculums. Publishers invest a lot in these curriculums and pay highly skilled educators to develop them. Just because you don't like a certain section of the curriculum doesn't mean it's not high quality. When a teacher decides she wants to leave out a segment of the curriculum she doesn't like, her students miss out on a specific aspect of instruction and now the teacher is at risk of sending an entire classroom up to the next grade level.

For instance, some teachers don't spend enough time breaking down and decomposing numbers in kindergarten or first grade. After a month on 10s, some teachers (understandably) get bored and move on because they have a lot to cover. However, if they push through too quickly, young students in particular who don't completely grasp the concept are at a deficit, especially to those whose teacher spent the appropriate time on that part of the curriculum—and then the grade level above has to work double hard to catch them up.

I struggle with this issue as a leader. I want to make sure that my teachers can use their skills and what they've learned in their years of teaching, but I also want to make sure that we cover everything with the same vocabulary and emphasis.

While we want teachers to be creative and to use what they know about their own individual classrooms and what they've learned through years of experience to enhance their class, we also need to make sure that an entire grade level receives the same content with the same emphasis. This is a difficult task that must be the focus of a school and a grade level.

My policy for teachers is to think of the curriculum as a recipe. If you're a new chef, it's best to follow the recipe exactly as it reads. If you've used that recipe before or you're a gourmet chef, you know how to make the dish taste good to picky eaters, or to make it edible for vegetarians. But if you deviate too far from the recipe, suddenly you've got a shrimp salad when you set out to make pizza, and that's a problem. If a teacher wants to move away from district or school exceptions because he thinks something will work better, he must be able to back this up with positive data results.

I've been blessed with fantastic teachers, so I give them a whole lot of autonomy. If they tell me, "We've done this for years and we believe we know what's best," then I say, "I'm okay with that and I support you, but FYI, the district will assess us on fractions on December 12, so you need to be ready for that."

Sometimes parents have issues with the canned curriculum, but for different reasons. The way kids learn math, for instance, has changed a lot from when we were kids. Instead of learning by rote, younger children in particular are taught core concepts and number sense. This approach can upset parents who think the way they were taught was the one true way or frustrate those who don't understand the new educational method.

This situation has happened with me. I went to visit family in Houston some time ago and tried to help my nephew with his third grade math homework. He used something called the forgiving method of division, which I'd never heard of before. It sounded like something from couples' therapy. I was inclined to go back and teach him the way I had learned, but fortunately he was smart and patient enough to explain this new method to me. It takes longer than the way I learned, but eventually it became clear to me that, with its emphasis on students making estimates and then checking their work, it's a better tool for teaching children number sense than just memorizing multiplication tables.

At Liberty Elementary we offer family nights to explain to parents how their kids learn, and I think more administrations should step up, even if it's just to encourage teachers to send a note home that reads,

"Please understand that your child may learn differently than you did." Many parents need to be reassured that they're intelligent, and there wasn't necessarily anything wrong with the way they learned. Think back to when parents were taught to put babies to sleep on their stomachs versus what they're taught now, or how car seat regulations have changed over the years. It's not an indictment on the old way—it's simply a new method that's come out based on evolving information and research.

Sometimes parents are just plain embarrassed when they try to help their kids with their homework and don't understand the assignment. As long as you made a good-faith effort and worked with your child, without TV breaks and distractions, you shouldn't feel ashamed to send a note back to school that reads, "We worked on this for 45 minutes and were frustrated. Can you help?" A teacher would much rather help a parent than have to reteach a child. I think of those parents who believe it will give their three-year-old a head start to teach him to write his name, only to start him off with poor writing and letter formation.*

Never be ashamed to ask for help. The only time a teacher gets upset is when it's the 14th time that month that his homework was incomplete, and the teacher knows the child was at soccer tournaments all week instead of doing schoolwork. In that case, no curriculum on earth will help your child get caught up.

---

*BTW parents, if you truly want to help your child with writing, you need to focus on helping your child master only three things: drawing a straight line from top to bottom (I, like the base of a capital T), drawing a slant from top down and right to left (/, like the right base of a capital A), and a correct curve (basically a capital C). If your child comes to school having mastered these three formations, he will master his letters easily and quickly.

8

ASSESSMENTS

A Necessary Evil, or So I Am Told

I have developed an assessment for government leaders called the W.I.A.K.A.R.. Don't you think it's fair that if our students have to take a state assessment every year then our politicians should also have to take one?

W.I.A.K.A.R. stands for:

What
I
Actually
Know
About
Reality

The first set of W.I.A.K.A.R. assessment questions is passage-based: "This is a story called Martha the Cake Maker and Billy the Guy That Don't Know Nothing About Baking." Politicians read the story and have to decide who would be better to call on to make decisions about baking: Martha the professional or Billy who don't know nothing. The politicians get extra credit if they can figure out the allegory in this story, and a gold star for spelling A-L-L-E-G-O-R-Y correctly.

Then the W.I.A.K.A.R., of course, includes multiple choice questions:

When funding is needed for education, what's the best thing to do?

    a. Sell all the band and orchestra instruments and use that money.

    b. Cut the arts, because don't nobody need to know their colors anymore.

    c. Freeze teachers' salaries for 14 years.

When school A is closed but school B is overcrowded, how do you get the funds to bus school A students to school C?

    a. I don't know, but check out this really funny bet I made with our neighboring town over who will win the big football game later this month.

    b. I don't know; my kids go to private school. At least, I assume that's where the nanny takes them.

    c. I don't know, and if you don't leave right now I'm going to call golf course security.

Don't you think that's going to give us some good information about what our politicians believe about education? I hope that all the states will adopt the W.I.A.K.A.R. for our government leaders. We can even announce politicians' scores in the newspaper. I can predict what their scores are going to be, but let's do it anyway.

I'm not exaggerating when I say that some teachers leave the profession because of all the assessments they have to do.

They get assessment stress from all directions: the district, which needs to hold all the schools accountable; principals, who want to hold the teachers accountable; and the state, which oversees the educational system.

In my opinion, it's too much—at all ages. You've got kindergartners taking an assessment during the first week of school, when some of them have never sat in front of a computer. Even at Liberty, I think we're overassessed: we lose four weeks of instruction per year due to universal screeners and state testing, and many schools lose five or six weeks of instruction due to required assessments.

Some systems require a weekly or even daily look at assessments. That's another stressor for teachers because sometimes a week isn't long enough for students to grasp a concept. On top of that, most teachers feel assessments don't tell them anything they didn't already know.

It's also beyond ridiculous when we're required to test students with huge academic needs—who have been identified as having a learning deficit—with the same assessments as their "on grade level" peers. I wish more politicians could understand the stress and ridiculousness of having to give a sixth-grade test to a student who is reading at a third-grade level.

Allegedly, assessments are necessary because you want to see that the instruction in the classroom is effective, and that's logical. But universal screeners, which test everybody at the same level, often don't match the teacher's instruction. Instructors get aggravated when they sit at a computer lab and watch students struggle through a state- or district-level assessment, aware that it's not content that was covered. And there's no consistency between assessments. We have one curriculum that teaches the word "tradition" for family culture while another assessment uses the word "customs." Sometimes the words "compare" and "contrast" are used differently. "Compare" might mean "find both similarities and differences." Sometimes it only means "find the similarities."

All this inconsistency leads to frustrated kids and frustrated teachers.

Ideally, teachers would create assessments themselves because they know what the students have been taught. Instead, you've got companies like Pearson and Houghton Mifflin publishing them. States buy these tests from curriculum companies, and of course curriculum companies gear assessments toward their own products because they want schools to buy their curriculum, and if you buy their curriculum then you're gonna do better on their test.

The current logic in the United States is that if we just assess students more and with more difficult content, then teachers will teach at a higher level. That's not what happens.

Depressingly, I don't know what we can do to change the current assessment reality aside from schools just figuring out the most practical way to handle them when they come. In the meantime, politicians opine, "This school's failing" or "This school's an F; that school's a D," when they've never actually stepped foot in that school. They don't know schools' struggles or their funding issues, yet they throw data in teachers' faces that ultimately wipe out school staffs and administration based on very little knowledge. We're not gonna change the fact that politicians who don't know anything about education are the ones who make decisions—as long as we keep voting them in.

I tell teachers that maybe they *should* leave the profession if they can't come to grips with the reality of assessments. Top down, you're always gonna have politicians overly reliant on test scores, because that's all they know. It's the nature of the beast in education. Ultimately, you just have to be able to lay your head down at night and say, "I did what was best for these kids. I instructed them in the best way that I could, and whatever happens, happens."

Sample Script for Leading Kindergartners through Assessments

All right, kindergartners, today, we're going to take a computer assessment and I know you're going to . . . what? "Assess." It's a test.

Today we're going to take a computer test, so you can show us what you know on this computer. Look, we're just going to play a really fun game, okay? So, it's—

Why you taking off your shoes? Seriously? I don't care if you take your shoes off when you play a computer game at home. Put your shoes on, okay? Somebody help him tie his shoes. Anybody know how to tie your shoes? Susie, your mom thinks you're gifted—get over there and try to tie his shoes, okay?

Here's what we're going to do. Today, we're going to take a compute—No, you can't touch the screen. It's not that kind of computer, okay? Here's what you're going to do, okay? You're going to take this mouse right here and you're going to use—

Yeah, no, it's not that kind of mouse. It's a computer mouse. It's not going to bite you. So, you're going to use this mouse. No, it's not the kind of mouse that's in your grandma's basement. Let's say it's a clicker.

You're going to use this clicker right here and you're going to take these two fingers and you're going to put them right . . . no that's not what your mama means when she says don't use your middle finger. This is okay to use your middle finger, okay? So, you're going to use—No, your mama's not going to take away cartoons if you use—

You know what, we're not going to use our middle finger. We're using this right here. We're going to use our pointer finger right here and put it on the—

Okay, look, it's a clicker, not a mouse. And we're going to use our . . . okay, I know what you do with that finger but we're not going to call it that okay? We're going to click it right here. I don't care if your mama calls it that, we're not going to . . .

Okay, look, you're going to use your nose-picking finger on the clicker to take your computer test. All right? So, when you find . . .

No, you can't go to the bathroom. We just went to the bathroom two minutes ago, all right? What do you mean you didn't have to go then? It was two minutes ago. Okay, just go. Go to the bathroom.

Okay, you're going to use your nose-picking finger on the clicker and you're going to look. Now I'm going to do the first one for you, okay? Let's do what it says.

You see this boy right here? He's holding something. Look at what he's . . . yes, it's a boy. So, look at what he's . . .

I know it's a boy, trust me, okay. It's—I don't know. He's got short hair, he's got blue shorts on, so, okay can we just agree that it's a boy?

All right, look at what he's holding. Okay, I see that Susie is a girl and she's got short hair and a blue . . . look, it's a boy. Just believe me. Stop asking about the boy. Look at what he's holding. That's what's important.

Now this sentence right here says, "The boy is holding up _____." No, he's not really holding a blank. How can you hold a blank? There's no—

Okay, let me read this sentence again to you. The boy is holding a "hmm." What's the "hmm"? Okay, no he's not really holding a hmm. Okay, look, look, we're trying to find a word here. He's not holding a blank. He's not holding a hmm. What is he holding?

Let's try this: he's holding a ball. So, the boy is holding a ball. Now you're going to look down here at the words that are down here and you're going to end up clicking with your nose-picking finger which one is the right word. Look for the word "ball."

A: Cat? No, that's not it.

B: Dog: No, that's not it.

C: Ball.

Okay, you're going to use your nose-picking finger on the clicker to click "C."

This is a C.

What do you mean you don't know what a C is?

Okay, you know what, this is giving me heart palpitations, we're not doing this. Let's get on outta here and go to recess.

9

SCHOOL RANKINGS
Look Beyond the Grade

When I arrived at Liberty Elementary in 2014, the Kentucky Department of Education had classified the school as "needs improvement." I remember when we learned about the 2015–2016 classifications, seeing the excitement of the teachers in the staff meeting as they waited for me to try to explain the various scores until they basically said, "Yeah, yeah—just skip to the last line. We want to know where we're at!" In one year, we had moved our state scores up to "proficient" and have steadily improved with each year. While these scores on state assessments are only a fraction (and I mean a *small* fraction) of a school's success, they are an indicator that our community and stakeholders look to when monitoring progress and success.

I attribute our improvement to the prioritization of positive climate and culture at the school. Wherever I've taught, my philosophy has always been to let the teachers teach and support them in any way I can, whether it's to give them the funds they need, step in to help with a parent that's taking up a lot of the teacher's time, or just not make announcements in the middle of the day.

My focus coming in was to be supportive and do everything I could to enable teachers to teach, and improved test scores would follow. My tactic was to ask every teacher, "What do you need?" If a teacher came in with a bag from the office supply store, I would say, "Where did you get that? Did you pay for that yourself?" If she said "yes," I'd ask, "Did you get a raise? Because if you didn't get a raise, I don't know why you spent your own money on supplies that we should be paying for." Whether it's paper and pencils or a Hello Kitty poster, I wanted to make sure we worked out our budget so that teachers had the materials they needed to teach. Simple things like that can affect overall attitude in a school; when teachers feel like their time is protected and their administration wants to support them, everything else falls into place.

This isn't common practice at every school. Obviously, many schools just don't have the money to support their teachers. But some don't even allow teachers free access to the school's supply closet, which floors me. My philosophy is, if you need something out of the supply closet, get it. That's what it's there for. They shouldn't have to go to the secretary and beg for staples.

A lot of principals believe in giving each teacher the exact same amount of money, but I don't think that's practical. For instance, a teacher requested a new classroom rug because hers was falling apart. That doesn't mean we'll announce, "Everybody gets a new rug," but we will give that teacher what she needs. It's like what teachers tell their kids: "Fair does not mean equal." All staff should be allotted some funding for their classrooms, but you should also make room for special requests from anyone.

However, as proud as I am of Liberty's improvement, I'm aware that ratings and rankings often don't represent the whole picture. If you're working at a school that is novice, not progressing, or whatever the category is for your rank, a lower rating doesn't imply that you're not a good teacher or administrator. There are fantastic teachers at all schools, but that can be overshadowed by a bad reputation in terms of behavior issues or infrastructure, even if the teachers work themselves to death to try to improve it.

I've taught at struggling schools and know that positive changes can be made even when the budget is an issue. During my first year in Lexington, I taught at a 100 percent free and reduced lunch school as a math interventionist, where I pulled struggling students out of fifth grade for extra help. There were a whole lot of behavior issues and the general attitude at the school wasn't great—I walked into that building and was greeted by kids who cussed at me and got into fights. And by the end of the year, guess what? They still argued and cussed and fought, but they were much better behaved for me than they were for other teachers. Why? Because those students were grateful for any kind of praise, which I was generous with. They simply weren't used to it, and neither were the parents. I'd call the parents personally any time I had good news, which meant a lot to them because they were only used to getting bad reports from the school. It's not like the kids suddenly started loving school and became model students, but I saw improvement because I took the time to build relationships.

Parents concerned about their child's school rankings need to zoom in on the smaller picture. Is your child successful? Is your child happy? That's the bottom line. You may say, "Wow, my school is only getting a D?" That doesn't mean your child is in a D classroom with a D teacher. It just may mean overall there are a lot of big-picture struggles. Check in with your child and see if he's happy. Get involved and support the teacher—change can begin with you. The bottom line is, do you feel that your child is progressing, that your child is learning, and most importantly, that your child is happy? In the end, that's what matters.

It's not a level playing field out there, I know. I grew up what I consider poor. My parents didn't want to spend the money on a science fair board, so they tracked down a spare refrigerator box and cut the board out themselves, which was mortifying for me. There are many students out there who come from struggling homes, whose parents live from paycheck to paycheck. Not everyone can sacrifice the time to be a room parent. Those parents who never seem to donate snacks to the class party aren't lazy or bad parents—it's often just life circumstances. When you work three jobs to make ends meet, reviewing your child's math work every night is not a high priority. When you're in foreclosure on your home, your cellphone's been cut off, or you don't have electricity, buying extra school supplies for the teacher is just a nonstarter. These types of life situations, humanity situations, are often at the root of lower school rankings.

The grass is not always greener on the other side. I think there's tremendous pressure that comes with being a highly ranked school. Every school has areas that are stronger than others, so it's not like we get a good rating and feel like we can just rest—there's pressure to improve even more. It's much easier to move a student from a 40 to a 50 than it is to move a child from an 80 to a 90.

Plus, highly ranked schools often come with highly involved parents—helicopter parents, who bring in huge expectations for their children's success. There's the straight A student whose parents think he should be moved into the gifted and talented program. There's the parent who feels compelled to keep up with the Joneses, whose child informs which fifth grader had a limousine pick up him and 60 of his friends for his birthday party.

So yes, great rankings are encouraging, and lower rankings can be a morale killer, but from an administrative perspective, regardless of rank, you can still support teachers to the best of your ability, learn to share good news as well as bad, and practice empathy. And to you parents, a child's success in life probably isn't based on a great school rating but that she's raised by people who know her, love her, and try their hardest.

PART 3

MEALS, SNACKS, AND OTHER "DERLICIOUS" THINGS

10

LUNCHTIME
Don't Bring Me No Lunchable to Open.
Just Don't.

People often ask me what the most stressful part of the beginning of the school year is. That's an easy answer. It's kindergarten lunchroom duty. See, kindergartners have never been together in a big ol' group, trying to eat lunch. It's like trying to get a bunch of kittens to do something. You get one seated down and then another one's under the table and then the one you seated down is gone and they're licking your hands and they're all over the place. It's just crazy.

And then there's Lunchables. Now, I know these are tasty treats in little compartments, but they are a lunchroom duty nightmare. If parents bought these once, you just open up once and there's little circles of bologna and the kids eat them, that'd be fantastic. But unfortunately, they get these fancy ones. Then I get, "Open my Lunchable. Will you open my pizza sauce? Will you open my pepperoni? Will you open my Capri Sun? Can you open my Nestle Crunch?" It just ends up being crazy.

Then, kindergartners get very excited to talk to you, and they do this, "Um, um, um, um, um, um, um, um." And you sit very patiently waiting, and then they say something so off-the-wall and random, you don't know how to answer, "Um, um, um, um, my grandma's got six toes on one of her feet." True story. And then I just say, "Your grandma is so fancy."

And lastly, kindergartners wanna be your best friend. They are so wonderful. I love them, but I do not have time to debate whether a pony would be a good inside pet while I'm trying to open 47 Lunchables. These are some things I actually had to say during one single 20-minute kindergarten lunch room duty:

Get that out of your mouth.
Get that out of your ear.
Get that out of your nose.
You better not have swallowed your tooth.
Yes, I know I have a big belly.
No, you cannot die from eating too many sweet peas.
Why you trying to drink two milks?
Quit spinning in your seat.
I don't have any butter in my pocket.
No those are not real diamond rings.
Why is your shoe on your tray?
Your teacher is not a werewolf.
Yes, I would be scared if a Tyrannosaurus Rex came into the
    cafeteria.
Your brother did not invent Skittles.
I love puppies.
I love kittens.
I love donkeys.
Yes, I think it would be fun to ride a giraffe.
Yes, I'm very scared of loud noises.

I'm telling you, if you wanna know stress in your life, come volunteer for kindergarten lunchroom duty.

When I was a child, my dad worked as a PE teacher and supported our family of four on $16,000 a year, while my mom stayed home with us. We were too poor to afford a 25-cent lunch, but too rich to receive free and reduced meals. So I brought the same thing for lunch to school every single day: a bologna sandwich, two cookies, and chocolate pudding that I tore the label off, because it was Thrifty Maid brand (we couldn't afford Del-Monte) and I was embarrassed to be seen eating Winn-Dixie's brand of pudding. If we had an extra 25 cents, I got to eat lunch in the cafeteria, and it was a huge, special occasion. Even better was when I got to be the table cleaner for the day—if I helped wipe up after lunch, I could go back and get some extra dessert. My well-established love of free and unexpected treats at school goes back a long way.

For most children, lunch is a fun break in the day to eat, socialize, and maybe enjoy a treat. For teachers, however, especially the first week of school, lunchtime can be like herding cats, between the students' excitement and the little ways parents can, unknowingly, make lunchtime more complicated than it needs to be.

Parents, here are some do's and don'ts for lunchtime in order to make it pleasant for your kids, their teachers, and staff.

DON'T overdo it. I'm absolutely amazed when a child comes to school with a suitcase full of food. I don't know how in the world the parents cram that much stuff in a small bag—stuff the kids don't eat. Please believe me that your child's not going to eat as much at school as she eats at home. The kids have 25 minutes, and they socialize for the majority of that time. Kids could go into the cafeteria and not eat a thing and be okay with it. There is no way they'll have time to eat everything if you put more than three things in a small child's lunch.

DON'T pack complicated items. Before you pack your child's lunch, ask yourself, "Can my kid open this Thermos himself?" "Is he dexterous enough to work all the parts of this Bento Box?" Have him practice at home, seriously, even if you think your kid is old enough to figure it out. Take a Saturday and make sure your child can pour the soup from the Thermos to the cup. See if she can stick her own straw in a Capri Sun (this should be on state testing). The cafeteria people are there to help in any way they can, but when there are 150 kids, and half of them kids need help with their lunches, then it's a huge scramble.*

DO send notes in your child's lunchbox. Kids love that, and the cafeteria monitors do as well. As much as the staff might be driven to distraction having to open a ton of thermoses (thermi?), they do love to help kids read notes from home. However, cafeteria monitors don't silently award points to parents who pack the most thoughtful lunches. Sometimes I laugh about how lunch in August compares to lunch in May. In the fall, you've got heart-shaped sandwiches and vegetables in little color-coordinated compartments of Tupperware. By the end of the school year, you've got a Ziploc baggie full of Cheerios and a whole carrot that's not even been peeled. No judgment.

DO let your kid learn consequences. There are those days when kids forget their lunch at home. I don't think it's your job to run to school when it happens. There's no reason why children can't eat school lunch. We have parents who say, "Oh, my child won't eat that." Well, the bottom line is, kids can go without lunch if they choose not to eat, and if they're hungry, they will eat what they're given and if not, they won't starve.

DON'T pack your child Mountain Dew, Red Bull, or other sugary drinks. You would be floored by how many people send a Red Bull in

---

*Parents who request that their child's lunch be heated up in a microwave should be fined $500. Just sayin'.

with their kid—some will even sneak soda into their child's water bottles, either because it's simply what they grew up with or because the parent just cannot say no. Many times, though, when we call a parent about her child bringing that type of drink to school, she'll say, "Oh no, I told him not to do that," and it turns out the child has snuck into the pantry, grabbed a Red Bull, and stuck it in his lunch box, because he thinks it's cool. In general, elementary school children shouldn't drink soda, period, and particularly not at school when a sugared-up kid is about to be returned to his poor unwitting teacher.

DO let teachers know if your child finds lunchtime stressful. When I was a child, I remember holding my breath for those days when the teacher would say, "Okay, today you can sit by whoever you want to." I recall the excitement of standing in line without my teacher there, and how I could talk to the people in front of me and behind me, which I couldn't do in the classroom or in the hallways. However, some kids are the exact opposite. If that's your child, tell his teacher or counselor, "He has a very hard time socially, and says he doesn't have any friends to talk to at lunch." Teachers are excellent about lunchroom table assignments. They know exactly which kid needs to sit where. They mull these scenarios over constantly: "Who is gonna sit and not say two words? Who's gonna sit next to Bonnie, the talkative girl who will chat with anybody?" If you give the teacher a heads-up that your child may struggle with lunchtime, odds are she'll have a solution in mind.

DO follow the cafeteria rules, even if you think they're unreasonable. We don't allow parents to bring McDonald's in to the cafeteria, yet sometimes we have those who sneak it in, and then we have to pull their child out of the cafeteria to eat in the conference room, and then we have to remind parents not to do that again, because it's disruptive. We also sometimes have an issue with our open-door policy in the cafeteria—while we welcome parents to come in occasionally and eat with their children, the rule is that the kids can't bring friends over— yet we have parents who break that rule. "It's ridiculous that I can't bring my child's best friend over. I'm gonna let my daughter invite Suzi and Billy to sit with us too." Well, you don't understand, Mom, that we've got two tables for parents and we've got 12 seats and we've got 24 kids. If everybody was to come in and invite a friend, it disrupts the seating arrangement and also creates issues where some people feel left out. Schools don't create lunch rules to torture parents. The next time you think a school rule doesn't seem to have any value for you or your child, try to consider the other 599 children in the room and the people who watch them.

DO NOT use lunch as a time to prank your child or otherwise potentially embarrass him in front of his friends. I can't believe I have to say that, but it happens. I remember when my dad packed my lunch one time and he warned, "Don't look until you get to the cafeteria—I packed a special surprise." And he had put a Gains-Burger—a dog food burger—in there as a joke. I thought it was funny, but it could have traumatized me if I was a sensitive child. We have a friend who thought her high school son would *love* it if she brought in a Crock Pot of Sloppy Joes every year for his birthday—just what every teenager wants, right? We've literally had parents who want to come into the cafeteria dressed as a clown. Even if your big, hilarious idea might actually be funny to your child, it can seriously disrupt lunchtime, so save it for after school.

But Wait! Teachers Eat Lunch, Too

There are some aspects of school life where there are parallels between teacher and student lives, and a great example of that is lunchtime. Just as there are rules for parents to make lunch pleasant for everyone at school, I have guidelines for teachers on how to use lunch break as an opportunity to improve overall attitude at your school:

DO socialize at least once a week. There's no reason you should have to eat with your team every single day if you don't want to, or if you need the time to grade papers. However, it's a climate and culture issue when your entire team eats lunch together and you never join in. Once a week, eat with your colleagues for at least 15 minutes before you go back to grading. I'm sorry, I know some of you are rolling your eyes and saying, "Gerry, my lunch break is the only 20 minutes I have to myself all day." But I'm telling you, everybody has to take responsibility for camaraderie.

DO try to keep lunchtime conversation light and positive. "I eat with this group of teachers and all they do is complain." I've seen a lot of staff move out of group lunch scenarios because of negativity. These are opportunities for better communication. If there's a source of constant negativity during your teacher lunchtime, I think it's fine to pull someone aside and say, "You know, this is stressing me out: lunch is supposed to be when we get to know each other, and all we seem to do is complain. Can we try to keep the conversation lighter?" Venting is understandable sometimes, but not every day over your 25-minute break.

DON'T bring a green liquid shake as your lunch. Because nobody wants to see that.

DON'T bring salmon, tuna, or any other kind of stank fish in and put it in the microwave. There is nothing more to say.

DO take the time allotted for lunch seriously. If you're supposed to drop your kids off at the cafeteria at 11:15 a.m., you need to walk in the door at 11:15. You don't need to come in at 11:12, because now someone has to monitor your kids when he shouldn't have to. And don't come at 11:17, because then you're backing up the class behind you. Same thing with pickup: if you're supposed to pick your kids up at 11:45, be there at 11:44, because somebody has inevitably spilled something, or argued, or cried, or is in the bathroom. I know that most teachers have only 25 minutes for lunch, but to arrive on time is to be late for those little things that require extra attention. I wish I could require chronically late teachers to perform lunchroom duty, because when they're late, they have caused tremendous stress for our paraprofessionals.

And DON'T use the principal or a parent as an excuse for being late to pick up your kids. If I, a principal, am talking to you, I have no clue what time you're supposed to be in the lunchroom. If I stop to ask you something at 11:44 and you're supposed to be at the cafeteria at 11:45, you need to say to me, "I gotta go get my kids." Same with a parent: "I know this is extremely important, and I want to finish this conversation, but I've got to go to the cafeteria. I will call you right after school. I promise."

DO have administrators perform lunch duty. Despite how crazy it makes me, I spend the first weeks of school on kindergarten lunch duty, which is where my lunchtime video came from. The kinder-gartners, I say with love, know nothing, so we triple up duty for the first two weeks of lunch. This is a learning time for the kids, but it's also a learning time for administrators to see the flow of things, the mistakes. Perhaps the milk line needs to be moved farther away from the trash can, for instance. Plus, the students see you when you're in there, which is why I think administrators should regularly walk through, even if they don't speak to anyone. You can get on the announcements and say, "I'm watching you in the cafeteria." You may not have actually seen anything, but it can't hurt if students think that at any moment the principal could show up.

DO have counselors sit in on lunch duty once a week. There's no better way to read a kid's behavior than at lunch. A child can fake it in a 25-person classroom, but there's nowhere to hide when they're in the cafeteria and no one's talking to them. The very first week of school, my daughter came home from 11th grade and said, "I didn't have anybody to eat with." All of her friends were in foreign language classes, and they had lunch opposite from when she did. That's devastating to hear as a parent. I stressed and prayed over this nonstop until a few days later when she came home and said, "I have lunch with all my friends now. They had more kids at one lunch than the other, and they changed all the foreign language classes to go to lunch at the same time as me." That was a huge relief to me as a parent, and prompted me as an administrator to think, "Gosh, I hope that every kid has someone to talk to." As a parent, I hoped that somebody would walk by and observe my child at lunch with nobody talking to her, and school counselors can be that person.

DO remember the importance of cafeteria workers. I always say the people who get paid the least are in charge of the most stressful parts of school, and that includes the people who work in the cafeteria and who drive the buses. I know lunch workers deal with a lot of disrespect. The kids argue with you or roll their eyes at you. But lunch ladies are pivotal in making the day of a student, because they are often the first professionals to see a student during breakfast, or the first ones to communicate with children about potentially stressful situations. You'll have parents who call in and say, "My child is supposed to get a reduced-price lunch, but he won't go through the cafeteria line because he doesn't want to deal with the lunch lady." It's not really a kid's fault when he doesn't have his lunch money, but when the cashier yells at him because his parents are $11 behind, that makes the child feel bad about himself, or his parents. A simple gentle reminder with a "sweetie" or "darling" can get the message across instead of barking at someone, "Tell your mom!" Then kids think, "Well, you know what? I'm five years old. I can't remember what I did in the classroom 10 minutes ago, and now you're gonna tell me to tell my mom, who is my authority figure, that she needs to send in a check for lunch? Okay."

Kids sometimes get sick to their stomach, or spill, or start to eat their spaghetti in the lunch line. Well, guess what? That's age-appropriate behavior. Instead of screaming at a kid, try to understand when the child in question is just hungry or excited to eat something she likes—there's a reason they're behaving that way. A negative cafeteria worker is like a negative teacher—he or she affects the entire school. You're the lifeline to teachers or counselors if a child seems off or lately cannot afford lunch. The job of cooking food, serving it, managing a school's nutrition, and forging relationships with children are all extremely important.

11

ALLERGIES

Don't Let a Kid Go to the Hospital Because You Couldn't Come Up with a Peanut-Free Meal for Your Child

Parents whose kids don't have allergies don't understand how severe they can be, and it's frustrating when they don't pay attention to food requirements. I was one of those parents. I absolutely love peanut butter. As I write, there are no fewer than four jars of peanut butter in my home. So, you can imagine how irritated I was when I learned that I couldn't slap together a peanut butter and jelly sandwich for my kid's lunches just because some kid in their class had an allergy. *Couldn't they just take a shot or something for that? What do you mean I can't send in candy with red dye to a party? Am I really responsible for checking every little thing I send in?* The answer to those questions is a big, fat "YES." I was one of those parents because I was unaware of the seriousness of food allergies, and let's face it, basically I was selfish and lazy.

Some parents get mad when they send their child to school with food that contains nuts and we return the food home with the student. These parents don't get that what you send in could literally kill a child. They just see it as an inconvenience for them. "Well, I don't read every label. I didn't know there was peanut butter in the animal crackers." These parents don't realize that in the worst-case scenario, you can cause shock or even fatality because it was an inconvenience for you to insist your child eat something besides peanut butter.

We had a child at our school who had to go to the emergency room after the reaction he had when a restaurant server cut his salad with a knife that had previously been used to cut a peanut butter and jelly sandwich—even though the knife had been washed. Imagine how stressful that was for that child. Imagine being his parents, knowing that your child is in danger of a serious, fast-acting medical emergency and you have only so much control over what will send him to the hospital, and when.

We also deal with parents who say their children are allergic to things that they are not. One parent was mad at us because we had an egg toss at school; she told us that her daughter was allergic to eggs. Of course, this mother had no doctor's note, and it turned out that the parents *do* eat eggs at home—"we just don't let our daughter eat them." So, we can't have an egg toss at school, even though (a) your daughter is nowhere near the eggs, (b) is not actually touching the eggs, and (c) you can have eggs in your refrigerator that your child goes into every day?" They wanted us to go above and beyond, when they don't do that in their own home.

Parents, understand that we are deadly serious about our peanut restrictions. This isn't something we made up to be politically correct. It is real, and it is terrifying for parents, teachers, and the students who witness medical emergencies. If your child isn't allergic, be grateful and spend an extra minute looking at food labels. And if your child *is* allergic, and you want to get the entire school to change its policy about red dye or birthday parties, bring a note.

TWELVE AMAZING LUNCH ALTERNATIVES THAT ARE NOT LUNCHABLES OR PEANUT BUTTER AND JELLY

- hummus, cut up veggies, and crackers
- a can of Vienna sausages
- a box of Zebra cakes
- a jelly sandwich
- a cheese sandwich
- a turkey sandwich
- a ham sandwich
- just cheese
- just turkey
- just ham
- just bread
- literally anything*

---

* To be clear, anything without peanuts in it.

New! A Meal Plan for Teachers

Everybody always worries about school lunches, but I'm excited to introduce a meal plan I've designed exclusively for staffers. The brilliance of it is that it's free and when you're on it, you can eat every day! This unique plan is called "A or B: Eat for Free."

Here are the options:

Option A

1. Go into the staff lounge.
2. Open the refrigerator.
3. Take a picture with your phone of what's in there.
4. Three days later, come back and pull that picture up.
5. Whatever has not moved in teacher's fridge is FREE to eat.

This plan may look familiar to those aware of the "three-second rule," when you drop your biscuit on the ground and it's still good to eat if you pick it up quickly. If your food hasn't moved from the staff refrigerator in three days, it's fair game and if somebody ate it during that time, that's your own fault.

Option B

Tell your students that you're going to do a real-world experience and work on some project-based learning. It's all the rage in education these days.* Talk to your students about how you are a society and that you're going to impose a tariff on all imported lunches. Stand at your classroom door every day and say, "I need to collect the taxes on all lunches brought in." Have every student give you just a little something from their lunch. You might get a Dorito from one student, a Cheeto from another, and maybe a big old bite from a jelly sandwich from another. This way you can eat for free every day, and your students get a great lesson.

Whether you choose A or B, you win.

---

*Don't worry if you don't like it; it'll change next year.

PART 4

SPECIALS
Other Ways Kids Learn

12

SOCIAL WORKERS

Why Children and Parents Need Them More Than Ever

A Day in the Life of
Your Average Social Worker Doing Home Visits

"Hello? School social worker. Hello. Ma'am, I see you right there in them curtains. Open this door. Get over here and open this door. I see your shadow right here under the door. Open the door. Open the door! I see your eyes in the peep hole. I know you can hear me. Your child better be at school tomorrow. You heard me. That's right. If not, I'm gonna come over with the police and one of the ram rods. I'm gonna bust this door down and get 'em into school. That's right. You better be here. I know you hear me."

* * *

"Hello! School social worker! Honey, why you answering the door naked? Go put some clothes on. I'm serious. Ain't nobody got time for that. What do you mean you ain't got no clean

---

clothes? That's why you ain't been sending your kid to school? You know what, send your kid's dirty clothes to school and I'll wash them. Okay? What do you mean you can't afford to . . . You know what, you got a Range Rover right there in the driveway. I seen you picking your kids up in that Range Rover. Why don't you sell that Range Rover, then you can wash them clothes? 'The bus is always late,' that's why? No. The bus comes every single morning. Every single morning at the same time. And if they miss that bus, get in that Range Rover and bring 'em up. Turn some heat on. Get 'em over here. That's right."

* * *

"Hello! School social worker. 'Get off my porch or I'm gonna sic my dog on you'? Honey, this is the fifth time I've been over here. That dog's as big as my shoe. I'm going to put it in my pocket. Open this door. Ma'am, it's one o'clock. Why you still sleeping? It was too cold to get your kids up this morning? How about you sleep in your jacket and your jeans, and some socks. You can just pop out of bed and get 'em here. You'll be all warm. No, I will not excuse their absences if you give me a beer."

* * *

"Hey, I'm the school social worker, I'm just . . . What do you mean 'No hablo English'? You know English. You know what, I was standing behind you at the Golden Corral yesterday when you were arguing with that waitress about why there weren't no strawberry shortcakes. Don't tell me you don't speak English. Well, how about this? You understand this? Get your kid to school tomorrow. That's right."

* * *

"Hey, I'm the school social worker. I was wondering where your child's been the last week. Oh, you went to Disney World? You had to miss school for that? You got spring break in two weeks, you couldn't have gone then? Oh, it was cheaper to go during assessments? Okay. Oh, you worked on school work while you were gone. I'm sure you did. Like what, fractions? Okay, well how about this, your kid missed one week out of the last month. What fraction of instruction did they miss that they're not gonna be able to make up now? That's right. You need to do a better job next year of planning your vacations."

School social workers and counselors are so important. Today's children grow up in a world 10 times more stressful than what we ever dealt with, between overwhelmed parents, social media, and violence in schools. When you look at the history of school shooters, 90 percent of the time the perpetrators are children with psychological struggles and social-emotional issues, which is why the role school counselors play is more important than ever.

I realize that social workers and counselors are two different jobs and two different skill sets sometimes. But when it comes to school, often these two positions serve the same purpose: helping families and students manage their struggles daily. So, in this section I will use these two positions somewhat interchangeably.

A good school social worker or counselor understands the ins and outs of student behavior: how to help students with issues like academic frustration, bullying, body shame, sexual confusion, and anxiety over current events or divorced parents. We see children as young as kindergarteners come in now with strong emotional struggles. Teachers may be able to spot warning signs like a change in a child's behavior, but their focus is on instructional growth and improvement, which is why school counselors are so vital.

School counselors are the ones who hear little kids say things like "I'm tired; we slept in the car in the Walmart parking lot last night" or "Mommy was arguing yesterday, and somebody got hit." We certainly saw kids with behavior issues back when I was teaching in the early '90s, but it has become more overwhelming lately. It's no wonder we have first graders who flip tables out of anger when school shootings are in the news, 20-year-olds are raising five-year-olds, parents who work two or three jobs are stressed out and come home in a rage, and rich parents outsource their jobs to hired professionals 24/7—that's what kids pick up on.

Superior social workers meet with kids beyond school. I've worked with some who have followed kids through middle school, high school, and even college and show up at various graduations. We had one counselor here that helped a student get into an overnight academic program because his mother struggled so much. The counselor would visit the student on the weekends and take him shopping for school supplies in the fall. She kept up with him all year. That's a life-changing thing.

Our counselors are great about maintaining relationships with other school counselors. Many times kids who struggle emotionally or are in abusive homes move from school to school. It's not uncommon for our social worker to say, "I'm going over to Southern Elementary, so I can eat lunch with Suzy," because she's developed that relationship with Suzy and wants to set the next social worker up for success at Suzy's new school.

We get calls from the middle school counselors, and I'm sure the middle school counselors get calls from high school counselors, asking, "How did you deal with this kid? Because he's struggling." Then our social worker can say, "Okay, you've got him with a strong-willed teacher. That won't work. He needs to be with a loving teacher," or "You've got her with a teacher she can run all over. You've got to find her a teacher that's more strong-willed," or, "He works better with female teachers compared to male."

You can't pull out a report card or test scores to see what's really happening in a kid's life. Social workers have the insight to much more about the struggles that students and their families endure. However, as illustrated in the video I made about school counselors, often when a counselor calls the parent, Mom or Dad can be very defensive.

A counselor may say, "I'm calling you because your child is struggling. I'm concerned and want to work with you."

A parent then may hear, "I'm calling you because you're not a good parent."

And that's not the issue. Parents need to understand that counselors want to work with a parent and help their children, not judge. But some parents see it as a failure.

Parents should think of a school counselor as they would their own therapist—if you feel depressed, you'd see a psychiatrist, and if your marriage is in trouble, you'd seek a marriage counselor. Our school counselors provide insights for both parents and children to cope with big changes or emotions. I wish more parents would see the counselor as a resource and not a source of shame. There are grandparents and older parents, too, who don't see the need for social workers, because that's not how they grew up—but that's the point. Today's children don't grow up the way they did, so, yes, we do need those social workers.

If you see a drastic change in your child, use the counselor. The least he or she can do is give you some information to read and say you're not going through this alone, or let you know that while you may not like it that your teenager rolls her eyes and slams her door, it's age appropriate.

Counselors can provide help that a teacher can't. They offer not only different training and skill sets, but also a separate environment. A student is more likely to talk about his or her life in a quiet office than in the few minutes between classes. In the best of situations, teachers and counselors work well together so that students can receive the help they need without having to skip academics or fun social activities like parties or pep rallies. A counselor may pull a child into a "lunch bunch"—when a counselor or staff member gathers students together to eat lunch with them as a group—or just step aside with a child for two minutes to check in: "How's your day going?" "How did you and your mom get along this weekend?" "Did you get to school today without any arguments?" Teachers should recognize that the help a student gets will lead to a smoother, happier classroom, and not fixate on how the counselor may momentarily disrupt her math schedule.

I think it's a good idea when social workers educate staff on what they work on with kids—not only to impart to teachers (and cafeteria workers, PE teachers, custodians, and bus drivers) how they can spot signs of emotional trouble, but to clue staff in on what they do all day, because otherwise some teachers get angry and think, "Why don't you come and teach a class on bullying to my students? What do you do all day?" Teachers can sometimes fall into the trap that parents do, of getting stuck in a bubble in which they say, "I deal with 33 students while the counselor's there all by herself," but in reality, if she has one child from every classroom to handle, the counselor has 33 students to handle as well.

Here's something I know about counselors: They become very attached to their students, particularly the ones who struggle. They sometimes form a near-parental bond with the kids, gaining their trust as they talk about struggles they have in the classroom or horrendous things that happen at home. These counselors equip students with life-changing skills, like how to make friends or build resilience to get them through instances of bullying, or how neurodivergent kids can navigate a world that may look, sound, and feel different to them.

Our district is trying to put more counselors in schools, but it's a slow process. School counselors are more necessary than ever, and a tremendous asset to any school. It's to the benefit of all kids that administrators, teachers, and parents see them as tools and not distractions or judges of parenting.

13

SOCIAL-EMOTIONAL LEARNING
Positive Culture Starts with the Grown-ups

Principal's Tip: Negativity—Fight It with Nonsense!

Teachers, I know as the school year starts, you're going to encounter people who don't like the new curriculum, who don't like the new principal, who don't like their class. They don't like nothing. If you keep talking to the negative people, that negativity get all over you like white on rice. You don't want that, so I have a few sergestions:

When someone is negative to you, don't throw shade back at them. When they're complaining about the new curriculum, you might be tempted to say, "Well, if you like the old curriculum so much, why don't you marry it?" Instead, distract them with Fancy Adjectives.™ Like when they are saying something negative, you can just look at them and say, "Your hands are so dainty." Or maybe you could look at their feet and say, "Your shoes are spectacular." Fancy Adjectives will throw them off, thereby ending the cycle of negativity.

Right in the middle of a complaint session, say something crazy and offbeat, like, "I love to eat glue." Or "I wonder what would happen if I punched a tiger at the zoo?" Then, you can move on to something more optimistic, like how you hope somebody brings Zebra Cakes to the next Goodie Table Day, even if Goodie Table Day was just yesterday.

Go with horse blinders. If someone starts complaining, put your hand up to the side of your face. That way, you can't see the negative person, but also, like sergestions 1 and 2, this distracts the negative person and throws her off.

* * *

I hope you enjoy these foolproof methods of improving climate and culture at your school.

The Thing About Friendly Teachers Is . . .

Anytime you get a large group of personalities together, there's bound to be conflicts and catty remarks, and teachers are no different. A teacher from seventh grade may say, "Oh, sixth grade's not where they're supposed to be, so we're going to have to struggle to keep their kids up." The sixth-grade teacher gets wind of this and gets upset. The second-grade teachers may complain, "Why do those fifth graders roll their eyes at me and jump all over the place?" and the fifth grade teacher is like, "Well, that's age appropriate, and we deal with it, and there's no need to flip out the way you're flipping out about it."

Inter-teacher drama occurs when stressed out people get on one another's nerves and talk behind one another's backs. This conversation inevitably gets back to everyone else, and it has to be dealt with, which nobody has time for, so, more stress.

Several times I've had meetings with teachers to help them work things out with colleagues because they didn't just go to each other first. I don't mind sitting and hearing people talk things out. But if this type of behavior occurs a lot among teachers at your school, it starts to become pervasive, and then you have a climate and culture issue in your building. Eventually this trickles down to the students, and the parents pick up on it as well, making any sort of improvement difficult.

Aside from flattering another teacher with Fancy Adjectives, here are some ways teachers can keep negativity at bay:

Get Away from the Debbie Downers

We tell our students this all the time: we are who we hang around. If you hang around negative people too much, no matter how you may try to be the positive influence, too much time in a pessimistic atmosphere will inevitably affect how you feel about your job. You say, "Oh my gosh, the firemen just came in and did the best presentation," and that coworker may say, "Yeah, well, now we'll be behind in spelling because that supposedly fun presentation took away from my lesson plan." No matter how old you are, nobody likes it when someone yucks your yum. Even if it feels fun to sneak away and have little snide discussions with your coworkers, it's not a healthy way to bond.

Bust Up Teacher Cliques with Positivity

Just like with students, there can absolutely be teacher cliques—or what seem like teacher cliques. In my experience, what often seem like exclusionary groups are just people gathering over some common social interest—like a bunch of teachers who have kids in the same Girl Scout troop. If you're a teacher or staffer who feels left out, make the effort to find something in common. Surely one of you must binge-watch the same show or know what place in town has the best pizza, or can speak to the latest toy they've been confiscating from their students. And if all else fails, you may need to ask yourself whether it's you who is the Debbie Downer. Fun, encouraging, positive people don't often get left out. Make more of an effort to get to know your fellow teachers personally, even if you know you won't be best friends off campus. If you have to, leave a box of conversation starters or *The Book of Questions* in the break room in case you can't find something to talk about.

Vent about Students in Private

Every teacher has that one kid who drives him or her crazy—usually a student with a very different personality from theirs. An organized teacher loves an organized kid and will get stressed out when she has a child who can't find his pencil when he had it in his hand two seconds ago. If you've got a quiet teacher and a loud child that always wants to be the center of attention, they will butt heads. But teachers rarely dislike students; they dislike behaviors. All teachers want to see kids succeed, but when you have a student who constantly argues or refuses to follow directions, it gets to be stressful. In those situations, most teachers do a great job hiding their negative feelings—it's their job. Some later venting is understandable and necessary. However, teachers need outlets other than the staff lunch room to disparage their students. It's simply not professional to complain too much about a certain child. Plus, it can taint other teachers who may have that child in their class down the line, which isn't fair to that child. Find one person—a person who doesn't work at your school—who can be your confidante and listen to you complain about a particular kid, parent, colleague, or principal.* And then keep that there.

Channel, Distract, and Divert

I remember one kindergartener who was a center-of-attention child, always interrupting. I told her teacher, "You handle her so well." The teacher told me, "At the beginning of every single day, I let her come up, and I give her two minutes of carpet time to do whatever she wants. She'll sing a song, she'll do a dance. She gets the attention of the entire class, and then we move on. She loves it." The teacher was able to give that child what she needed in order to get through the day. You can do that with a pessimistic colleague—there's truth in my video about negative people. Offer compliments, change the subject, or practice random acts of kindness. Never underestimate the power of an unsolicited candy bar or Starbucks drink.

Have a Goodie Table Day

(If you don't know what a Goodie Table Day is, see page 142 and thank me later.) Honestly, maybe this is everything you need. I probably should have just put this first and skipped all the other advice.

. . . They Make For Friendly Kids!

We have a parent who eats lunch with her child in the school cafeteria every day, not because the child needs help or is anxious but the mom just wants to. This drives me crazy because lunch is meant to be socialization time for a child. Parents and grandparents are welcome to come

---

*As if you'd ever have a principal you'd complain about!

and eat with their children at Liberty up to once per week, but not for the first three weeks of school, because that's the time it takes for kids to get settled, learn how to stand in line, and feel comfortable with their new classmates. Self-sustainability is something kids have to practice and learn, and no matter how much a mother may miss her child or worry about him, he won't learn how to form his own social circle with his mother swooping in just because she's worried or bored.

Parents are often concerned about bullying, a feeling I understand all too well from my experiences with my children. My son Jared was a big ol' football player and still experienced bullying. Once when he was in ninth grade, he was in the locker room after football practice, unloading his stuff into his locker when this fellow player, a major bully, came up, took my son's stuff out of the locker, and took the locker for himself. My son was very passive about it; even though he probably had 100 pounds on the bully, he didn't do anything. He just took a different locker.

When I heard about this, I was devastated. I told my son, "You should have said 'That's my locker,' and pulled his stuff out of there. You should have grabbed his shoes and thrown them across the room." My son looked at me like that was the dumbest thing ever. He was like, "It's a locker, who cares?" Jared's not one to cause a stink, and he knew that kid for who he was—a bully whom nobody liked.

It wasn't a big deal to him, but it was a really big deal to me. But the bigger picture is that even though the whole incident bothered me a lot, it hardly bothered my son at all. He was more intelligent than I could ever be.

So, parents need to remind themselves that what may often tear them up may be an instant their child forgets in no time. They need to trust that schools are on top of bullying, from elementary up to high school. Of course, teachers need to be aware of the personalities in their classrooms, and parents need to monitor their children for personality changes that may indicate social issues at school, but overall, kids are more resilient, and schools more observant, than many parents think.

Of course, there will always be bossy children, but bullying and bossing are two different beasts. One child will say, "He's bullying me," when in reality his classmate is bossing, with a desire to take control of the situations like who plays what and with whom at recess. A lot of times those are kids who lack self-esteem and don't know how to handle friendship situations, but that's one of the things we work on with the school counselor.

I think bullying is more likely to happen among kids from different schools, say, through sports leagues, YMCA activities, or social media, where parents and teachers have less control. A girl told us that somebody posted a picture of her on Snapchat, where they used an app that made her look ugly by putting horns on her head.

When a situation like that arises, we make sure never to get the different sets of parents together, even if the victim's parents demand it. They may say, "I want to meet with the bully's parents," but then as an administrator you've lost control of that meeting, so we will alert parents to what's going on, but won't get them together.

Sometimes when a child is accused of bullying behavior, their parents become argumentative, saying, "My child would never do that," or "My child is just fighting back against a kid who was mean to her first." But 90 percent of the time, if we've told parents, "We just want to let you know this is an issue outside of school that has come up," the parents say, "Oh my gosh, I didn't even know," and are glad we told them.

What works well is calling the parents involved and offering a lunch bunch club, especially in those mean-girl situations. Once you get an adult involved in monitored conversations, telling kids about their own time in school and getting students to talk out their feelings, they're often able to see each other in a different light.

When it comes to personality clashes in or outside the classroom, parents need to trust that teachers are on it. We don't want them any more than a parent does.

14

READING INTERVENTION
Catching Kids Early
to Set Them Up for Later Success

I, a certified reading interventionist, want to share with you some great strategies I've developed for struggling readers.

The decibel strategy. This is when you speak louder and slower when a student is struggling. Get your mouth ready to really stretch that word. When they can't get a sentence out, just read it to the student loud and slow and it will totally sink in. "THE. PIGEON. WANTS. A. HOT. DOG." "THIS. IS. NOT. MY. HAT." This also works really good if you're in a foreign country and someone doesn't understand you. "WHERE IS THE BATHROOM?" "DO YOU SPEAK ENGLISH?" It never fails.

The quick read. Basically, if a student is struggling with a reading passage, you just read it real quickly for them and then send the kid back to their desk or their classroom so you don't have to deal with them anymore.

The Scary Granny (SG). If a student is struggling with reading, you just threaten to call the SG. "I know you know them words. I'm going to call your grandma. She's going to come in here yanking on your head if you don't get reading." It's a great motivator.

The real estate strategy. This is one of my favorites. If you've got someone that's struggling with reading, you just check and see if they've moved. If they have, you can send them to their new district. That always works.

When I became an administrator, I was confident in the intermediate curriculum because I did most of my teaching for third and fourth grades. I was a pro at testing, grades, knowing what needed to be done to make sure those students performed how they needed to, and knowing how to move a class to the next grade.

But when I sat in on class, I suddenly felt inadequate with primary. I remember having to ask what "hunking and chunking" was in a meeting. I just felt so stupid, thinking, "I'm a principal. I'm these people's leader and I don't know what it means when someone says to 'hunk and chunk' something." It sounded like a cooking technique. (For the uninitiated, it's a way for new readers to break down words.)

I decided to do some research and went through Reading Recovery Training, which is a national intervention program in which, over the span of a year, you work with students with somebody overseeing you and giving you feedback in real time. My training as a Reading Recovery specialist completely changed my thought process on intervention. It made me realize the importance of addressing each child's specific issues rather than lumping a bunch of struggling kids together even if they have very different reading issues. If you give a child the wrong intervention, it doesn't help address his particular needs. This training gave me a deep understanding of not only how students learn but what good teachers do to intervene when they struggle. This program helped me become an instructional leader rather than just an administrator.

At Liberty, we put every bit of money we can into intervention, especially in primary grades, because we know that if children don't get help then, it will be an even bigger issue as they get older. We are blessed in that we run our budget to keep a tremendous amount of interventionists on our staff. Now we have a state-recognized intervention program. We put in an application with tons of other schools and we were the only school that got a check mark in all 11 categories for intervention. We are now labeled as a "model school for intervention" from the Kentucky Department of Education, often hosting visiting schools who observe our system and learn from my amazing Response to Intervention staff.*

Our district requires that students who perform at the 25th percentile or below receive intervention, but we can provide intervention for our students at the 40th and below. At that point, it's not so much intervention as it is enrichment. If a student is in the 40th percentile, he or she would probably show up as an apprentice student, with just some deficits that need to be worked on.

We run our intervention such that parents with a student who is struggling in a certain area will get a note that reads, "Your child will be pulled for 20 minutes, three times a week for math intervention." However, parents sometimes freak out when we tell them that—but they shouldn't. If your child is in reading intervention, it's a good thing. Yes, you should be concerned if your child is struggling, but how great is it that he can receive that help? It's fine to express concerns to the teacher, but never, ever deny your child what the school says he needs.

---

* If you'd like to see what reading, spelling, and writing tools our lead reading interventionist has developed for Liberty, you can view them online at joshmorganconsulting.com.

That's a major issue we have. If your child had a broken leg, would you tell the doctor, "No, I don't want crutches for him"?

Some parents argue, "There's this stigma with special education." Well, guess what, there will be a stigma when your child is 19 and can't read. Trust the professionalism of your school and don't ever hesitate to ask questions like, "Why is my child struggling like this?" "Can you show me the data?" "What can I do to help him?" We're all in this together.

Also? You can stick your child on every computer reading program in the world, but there's nothing better than a parent who sits and reads with a child, because your child loves spending quality time with you. A parent can have conversations about a book that a program can't: "Oh my goodness gracious, what's going to happen in the story? Who will find the lost dog? I can't wait to see what happens in the next chapter!" You can model strategies to your children, like "Wow, that didn't sound right—let me try that sentence again," or "I need to slow down," or "You know what? I need to use my finger because I'm reading so fast that I'm missing words."

Anything that makes reading fun and not a burden is a good thing. Don't make it sound like eating their vegetables: "If you read for 15 minutes you can play on your iPad for an hour." If you're just reading *Harry Potter* aloud to your child at bedtime, that still counts. You're not forcing her to read, which might cause frustration and make her say, "I hate this. This is boring," and you're being the example.

Think about the books you loved as kids and share those with your child. We share food we grew up eating and traditions we grew up celebrating, and books should be the same.

I'm realistic that even with the best strategies and intentions, kids get frustrated by reading, and working through that is not always delightful. When you teach a child to read, it's like trying to chop down a big tree in your backyard. It's horrendously hard, but how great is it when it's done?

15

TECHNOLOGY AND SOCIAL MEDIA
A Double-Edged Sword

I hate social media. I know. I know exactly what you're thinking: how hypocritical. And it is. Social media has been a tremendous blessing in my life. Without it, I wouldn't have this platform. I wouldn't have been able to meet and hear from so many great educators and to express my support of educational issues. However, I can't ignore how detrimental social media can be to a teacher, classroom, grade level, and school. Social media needs to be used correctly and it also needs to be monitored regularly—for kids and for teachers.

Here's one example of when social media + schools can be positive: anytime you can use it to quickly communicate with school parents. We use newsletters, Facebook, websites, school apps, and mass calling systems to get the word out about fundraisers, theme days, athletic events, and days off. However, a variety of communication methods is key—not every parent has a computer or smartphone, which is why we don't want to rely solely on, say, Facebook.

Many teachers do have Facebook pages for their classrooms, which can be a fantastic way to share photos and stories from the school day, but the school needs to monitor those pages closely. There's nothing wrong with a post captioned "Here was our class party" or "Here's a child who dressed up as Harriet Tubman who did such a good job on her book report." But you need parent permission to post pictures of their kids online. Also, keeping that Facebook page means the added responsibility of monitoring comments, which may be more responsibility than overworked teachers need.

Otherwise, anytime a parent complains on Facebook, he or she is now complaining to all 25 parents. You may have two or three jump on the bandwagon and the teacher feels absolutely horrible. A post as simple as, "Gosh, there was a lot of homework tonight" can open the door to other complaints from parents. And as we all know, when you're behind a computer it's easy to misread statements as negative. It's kind of like driving: when you're in the car, you're more apt to be negative about other drivers than you would if you were face to face with that person. On social media, there's always one parent who will chime in with something negative. I highly suggest if you have a social media page for your classroom that you shut off comments or set the page so comments need to be approved before publishing.

I have called parents about negative Facebook posts. I'm careful not to dress them down or demand that they delete their posts, but instead to say, "I'm so sorry we've put you in the position where you feel like you can't come directly to us. If you have a concern, please come to me." This always works—I don't aim to make them feel bad, but I can tell they're thinking, "Why in the world didn't I just call the school?" or, more likely, "Why didn't I just keep that to myself?"

I find that parents will say that they were frustrated with the situation and didn't realize how negative it sounded. They just thought they were talking to their friends and didn't think of how the school or the teacher would take the comment. Ninety-nine percent of our parents want positive relationships with one another and the school because they see the need to work together. There's always going to be that 1 percent who will rip you apart, but the bottom line is you will never change that person. Sometimes you just need to let it go.

A major frustration with social media is when it involves parents who listened to their children and took them at their word rather than following up with the teacher when something might sound unreasonable or silly. I had a parent post on Facebook, "How stupid is it that the school has a new rule that kids can't run on the playground during recess. Isn't that what recess is for?" This caused several other jerky parents (that's right, I said it) to chime in with what they considered to be stupid rules. I called the mother and asked where in the world she got that information and she explained that her daughter told her they weren't allowed to run on the playground. I explained that the students were welcome to run on the playground except in the mulch area (this is the area where we ground our playground equipment) because it's often congested with students and there are lots of poles and pieces of equipment they can run into if they aren't paying attention or trip over while running. The parent completely understood the need for that rule when I spoke to her, but unfortunately, she caused a negative situation by assuming the information her child gave her was true, even though it was ridiculous.

There are times, of course, when teachers don't think social media through well—like when they friend parents, which gives the parents access to their lives in a way that might not be so smart. Sometimes a teacher will call in sick and then parents see a photo of her at a concert or basketball game and ask us, "Why is she gone, yet on Facebook, we see she's somewhere else today?" (The bigger lesson here, of course, isn't just about teachers friending parents online, but also common sense and honesty.)

We've also had issues when teachers post pictures of parents that they're dating, which isn't wise in several ways. It's unprofessional to date your classroom parent. Obviously, that's your personal life, but when you post on social media for the world to see that you're in a relationship with Billy's mom and Billy wins a science fair, parents will say, "Billy's getting special treatment because Mr. Smith is dating his mom."

Parents need to be more alert than anybody when it comes to technology and social media. I'm leery when kids get phones at a young age—I see children as young as second grade texting their friends. A lot of parents feel their kids need a phone because they want to know where their children are after school, but just know that when you give child a smartphone, you're opening him up to social media. You may say, "My child will never do this or that with her phone," but children are smart, and they will do whatever they want to do when it comes to social media if they've got a smartphone.

However, I understand that social media is a form of socialization for kids. That's how they communicate right now. Keep in mind that their group text, Snapchat, or Instagram is their version of hanging out at the drive-in or whatever you did at their age.

My advice? Prolong your child's phone-free life for as long as possible. I went through this with my brother and sister-in-law. They were stressing because my sixth-grade nephew wanted a phone. A part of me thought, "Yes, he should have one for socialization," but another part of me was like, "Oh my gosh, you're opening up a real can of worms." And we saw it right away—suddenly, he's a kid who's got his phone at the dinner table and who's upstairs in his room on his phone rather than down with the family. His parents did a great job of saying, "You can use your phone during these hours." Monitor the phone, and know what apps are on there. Yes, it's good to give kids a sense of privacy, but you absolutely need to know what YouTube channels they visit and what apps they use because there are people who use social media to prey on children—even if it's not in a sexual way. I've had kids at school bring in their parents' credit cards and buy swords and shields in online games, who get around filters to inappropriate sites. It's just the nature of how intelligent children are, the things they think they can get away with, and the things they actually do get away with.

I probably understand this stuff more than most principals and parents. I've taken down more than one video after realizing I'd uploaded some content that made people mad. One of the most popular videos I ever posted was called "Teacher Bumper Numbers," which made fun of those 26.2 bumper stickers people put on their cars after they run marathons. The video suggested bumper sticker numbers for teachers, like how many minutes we get for lunch and how many minutes we get for the bathroom. The very last one was 4,162, representing the number of times people have said to me, "You get your summers off."

That video got picked up by a jogging influencer who has millions of viewers, and then it went through media outlets like Diply. Many comments from noneducators were rude, saying, for example, "You get paid plenty," "You do get paid to not work over the summer," "You knew what you were getting into," and "Teachers make a lot more than mechanics."

It didn't bother me, but it started to bother the teachers, and I didn't want that, so I took it off Facebook—and I've taken other videos down for less. People will say, "That's ridiculous, you took it down for one or two parents." Well, I know what it's like to be a parent and I wouldn't want to feel offended by something my principal posted—unless it's a humorous video about parents who never turn in a field trip form all year. If you're offended by that, turn in your flipping field trip form.

Before I put up a video, I screen it for several people like my best friend or teachers who might say, "Wow, that's not going to go over well," or "You know, you need to think about that." I'm not afraid to put controversial stuff up, especially if it has to do with a lack of support for teachers, but I don't want an argument between teachers and parents or teachers and noneducators. I also just don't have time to monitor every one of the 3,000 comments I'll get on a video, so if they're heated, it's just not worth it. When I put a new one up, I will usually spend about an hour monitoring the content to make sure it's not too controversial, but that's it. I don't have much time to interact with the commenters because if you speak with one viewer, you have to speak with them all.

My personal focus on social media is to put out videos, support teachers, and try to be funny. It's not to monitor comments, comment back, or email. I understand how much time I have to put in as a principal and I don't let social media in any way, shape, or form get in the way of that job.

16

GIFTED AND TALENTED PROGRAMS
Be Careful What You Wish For, Parents

If I could, I would change the name of the gifted and talented (GT) program to something more neutral, something that doesn't imply that other children aren't gifted or lack talent. These kids are just differently abled. Some kids are delayed; some are advanced.

At Liberty, a teacher typically requests a student evaluation for GT sometime between kindergarten and second grade, with the programs beginning in third grade. These kids get a curriculum that responds to their desire to solve challenging problems with hands-on activities in whatever area they're gifted and talented in (such as music, dance, math, or reading).

There's a lot of confusion over the difference between a successful student and a gifted student. "Gifted" is a specific, testable attribute, meaning that the child has enhanced academic abilities in a specific area. But many parents think that their child should go into GT because the kid makes straight As or studies hard, which is not how it works. For us, the student has to be in the 98th percentile of testing, and that is very rare. Many of our straight A students who are in the 95th and below will be completely successful at life, but they're simply not at the intellectual ability of the top 98th percentile.

It's no surprise that many parents request the evaluation regardless of whether their child is gifted. Most parents think their child is gifted in *some* way, and I see the issue of competition rearing its head in parent social groups where one child is in GT and another child's parent starts to feel a certain way about it. I remember when my kids were in school, a particular cohort of kids would always win the science fair. They truly loved science; nobody cheated or anything. We parents would joke about working hard on our science fair projects when we already knew who was going to win and go on to the next level. That type of comparison is natural. "Is that child smarter than mine?" "Are those parents better than me?" "Our project was good. What's going on?"

But every child comes with his or her own challenges and that's no different with gifted kids. It's not like your GT kid is guaranteed to become the next Mark Zuckerberg and will buy you a house in the next five years. Plus, many GT kids struggle with text anxiety or social issues. When they're identified as gifted, the world begins to respond to these children in a different way. Parents are often harder on those kids than they might otherwise be, like when the student doesn't make straight As or displays age-appropriate organization or behavior issues, like refusing to practice the violin. These parents are often hyper-involved and cannot hide their disappointment over any little setback. Then there are the kids who decide they don't like the GT program, who lose interest in the thing that they're gifted at. That's much harder on the parents than it is on the kids.

Unfortunately, I've also seen administrators abuse their power and push their own kids through the GT program. They may be straight A kids, but they're not gifted. All of a sudden, they're in a group of students who are more advanced than them on academic assessments, creativity, and deep thinking. Now they've been put in a new group, struggling, while their parents are happy because their child has been identified as gifted.

It's true that some gifted kids go on to become Rhodes scholars and receive full scholarships to great schools. And then you have the majority who become regular people like everybody else in the world. It's hard for parents to see the big picture when they invest so much in their kids, but as long as they love their children and are involved in their lives, it all pans out in the end.

17

BODY GROWTH AND DEVELOPMENT AND SCHOOL
When Private Parts Become Public

A parent I know recently got an email from her child's teacher informing her that her kindergarten-aged son and two of his friends were caught in the potty comparing their private parts. She was practically ready to cancel his birthday party, or call a therapist for him, or both. But as scary as it can be for a parent, kids' curiosity about bodies is age-appropriate, and we teachers deal with it all the time in some form.

Many parents consider body parts as a private thing. They may talk about it at home, but suddenly, their kids get up to a certain socialization age when they have time at recess or on the bus to start talking (or showing). Anatomical curiosity is not a sign that your child is horrible.

It's sad to me when I see a student whose parent clearly hasn't given him much knowledge about how his body works, or even the correct names for things. I taught fourth grade development classes, and I was just floored by the lack of knowledge students had, like boys who had never heard that hair is going to grow in certain places on their bodies. In those cases, it was often because they lived with parents or grandparents who didn't know how to talk about bodies and how they grow.

The flip side (although these things are not mutually exclusive) is when kids' caretakers allow them to watch R-rated movies or use the computer unmonitored, and they bring inappropriateness from home.

I think that society has made sexual conversations and situations completely acceptable at a much younger age than before. The music our students listen to is hyper-focused on sexuality and sexual activity, and our kids are introduced to types of videos, TV, and movies that we would never have dreamed of. Years ago, certain content couldn't be shown on TV until 10 o'clock at night. Now a child can pull something X-rated up on an iPad at 6 o'clock in the morning while Mom and Dad get ready for work.

My general advice is for both parents to be a little more aggressive when they talk to their young kids about body development and sex. You may not want to talk to your kindergartener about his or her growing body, but would you rather they get the information first from their friends—or from their friends' mom's phone?

By that same token, parents need to be more critical about what they expose their kids to. It sends mixed messages when we teach children to respect one another and each other's bodies and then let them watch mature YouTube stars, or play raunchy music in the car that objectifies women or glorifies casual sex. The people who make money influencing our students contradict the things that we want our kids to believe.

We do what we can at school, although there can be such a sliding scale of where students are in terms of maturity: we've got fourth graders with hair on their legs and ninth graders with none at all. It's not like fractions where we agree that most students are on the same page and this is the year to introduce this particular topic.

We've used a puberty curriculum published by Procter & Gamble that I liked. Of course, it was designed to promote and sell deodorant and tampons, but aside from that, it was a great curriculum that showed kids what's going on with their bodies. We'd send it home with the parents to get consent to teach it to their kids and if they liked, they could watch a video ahead of time. Most of the parents loved the curriculum because it enabled their kids to get information that's usually awkward to talk about.

I think parents trust us most of the time, although we occasionally get a parent who says, "My child never needed to hear this," and a teacher's thinking, "Why, yes, he did." In the right context, school can be a safe place for students to ask questions, and a better place to get that information than on the bus or during recess.

Growth and development education absolutely should begin at home. Parents need to be the first source, seeing teachers as helpful people tuned in to what students are talking about at lunch, during recess, and on the bus. Parents should always have a general idea of what's happening socially outside of school, in text messages, and on social media.

However, parents have to let go at a certain point. You can come in and sit with your child at lunch in kindergarten, but that's not happening by junior high. The only thing you can do is say, "We taught her how to make good decisions. We taught her how to resolve conflict. Now we have to trust that she'll follow through with that. If she doesn't, then it will be an opportunity for us to have a conversation."

We can't protect our kids from everything, and being a helicopter parent has its deficits. But you can be on top of what messages your children receive from the media, be in contact with their friends' parents, and let your kids know that you're involved. Advocate for teaching our students to be responsible, respect themselves, and care for other people. Everyone's kid will talk about sex, think about sex, and someday have sex. When it starts to enter kids' lives, you must trust that what you've taught your children will help them make good decisions, and there's really nothing else you can do.

PART V

THE PRINCIPAL'S OFFICE
What Makes It Run
and What Drives Us Crazy

18

THE PRINCIPAL IS YOUR PAL

Or Should Be, Anyway

INSIDE LOOK

Here are some things principals talk about when we get together at our principal conventions:

- How to make a 15-minute staff meeting last 45 minutes

- The art of sending out a mass email to everyone even though it pertains to only one person

- Ten ways to tell a parent her child is not really gifted

- What to do when an entire grade level is looking for you

- Calming the storms with jeans days and chocolate

All principals do things that get on teachers' nerves. I know this as a former teacher and because my teachers straight up tell me when I get on their nerves. They will come up to me and say, "You just wasted 45 minutes of our time when you could've emailed us." I tell them, "You're fired."

Just kidding. This type of feedback is valuable to me. As an administrator, I see myself as a lifelong learner. I made the principal workshop video to demonstrate that I don't always realize how I can do better, which applies to all principals. Sometimes teachers might be too nervous to tell principals what they really believe. This is why I talk about climate and culture so much. Teachers have to be able to go to the principal and say, as they've said to me, "When you're in my classroom for 20 minutes and you never speak up, I don't know if you're happy or sad. It would be great if you left me a note, sent me an email, said 'Great job,' or something, rather than just coming in and out, because I don't know what you're thinking."*

I truly believe, teachers, that if there's something you're struggling with, you need to go see the principal. It's gonna be awkward and the principal may not like it, but it's worse if you hold it in and never communicate. Then, tension gets to a boiling point and a good teacher will consider quitting, rather than have an awkward moment. When work consistently stresses you out, that affects your job, so you have to communicate that to the principal, whether it's a casual chat in the hall or a closed-door meeting, and let the chips fall where they will.

However, I know it's much more complex at a school than just "Tell your principal what's on your mind!" One thing I struggle with as an administrator is that sometimes, what's best for kids is not always what teachers want.

---

*Now I leave notes as often as possible (although I still forget on a regular basis. Just sayin').

For instance, sometimes a student is disruptive, and a teacher's response is to get him out of the room because that child is distracting 24 other kids.

That is an absolutely valid response. But when you send a child to the office, he misses out on instruction and won't receive a science or social studies lesson. Our goal as administrators is to get him back in the classroom as quickly as we can, because when he's in the office he's missing content. That's an example of when some level of stress is inevitable.

Another issue that comes up with administrators is handling communication with teachers. During my teaching years I had principals who I never saw except for the 15 minutes per year when they observed me. I try to make sure staff sees me regularly in the classrooms, not to look over teachers' shoulders but because I want to know what's going on in the classrooms, and I want the students to see that I'm aware.

Administrators need to find the right balance between nonexistent communication and overloading teachers to the point that they don't have time to work. If you send out too many emails per week, teachers stop reading. Information that needs to go out to everyone goes through me first so that I can include it in an email once or twice a week. This helps avoid overwhelming teachers with one email from the library, another from the PE teacher, and another from the cafeteria. We usually send out one school email on Mondays and then a shorter one on Tuesdays because we inevitably forgot something and need to follow up.

Being a principal is like being a parent. Before you become one, you have big ideas about what you will do differently and better than those who came before you. You go in thinking you will have the same opinions, control, or ideas that you had as an educator in the classroom. But then you get there and instead of handling just your classroom, you now deal with all grade levels and their content, plus specials teachers, parents, central office, budgets, and big-picture hiring practices.

You realize that principals have less control than teachers and parents think they do.

I'm proud that we have low teacher turnover at Liberty Elementary, and I think that it's because our staff is so supportive of one another—it's a tone we strive for in all situations. I think if more administrators adopted an "anything I can do to support my teachers" mentality and an "any feedback is valuable" perspective, they too could work with teachers who are happy 90 percent of the time. Okay, maybe 80 percent of the time.

19

SCHOOL OFFICE
The Brains of the Operation

An Average Five Minutes in the Life of an Elementary School Secretary

Erlymentary school secretary here. How can I . . . hold on one second, please. Hey, honey, why you late? Your daddy was pooping? No, don't write that down. Just put "Overslept" and tell your daddy to poop on his own time.

Erlymentary school, how can I help you? What time does your child have lunch? I can check. Who's your child's teacher? What you mean you don't know? What grade is she in? What do you mean you don't know? Are you sure you even got a child? Okay, you say it's a lady teacher. Well that really narrows it down. How 'bout this? When your child gets off the bus today, if you can figure out which one's your child, ask her who her teacher is, then call me back tomorrow.

Hey, honey, why you late? Write it down here. Traffic? Your mama told you to put "traffic"? There ain't no traffic. Everybody would be late if there was traffic. Put "Mama wouldn't get up" right here. All right, go to class.

Erlymentary school, how can I help you? What are we having for lunch today? Let's see: pizza, Go-Gurt, animal crackers. What do you mean you're gonna bring your child's lunch 'cause he won't eat that? Who's in charge at your house? I think he should be eating whatever we put in front of him. Picky eater? Well, okay if you have to, go ahead and bring his lunch up there. I'll write a note to the teacher. "Mrs. Cain, Snowflake's mama is bringing her son's lunch."

Hello, Mrs. Johnson, this is the secretary. I'm-a need you to take attendance. Yeah, every day. We do it every day. I'm not sure why you forget. You got your clothes on today? You could remember that. You should be able to remember attendance.

Erlymentary school, how can I help you? Whose mama is this? Steven's? Okay, you're going on vacation early? You wanna let his teacher know so she can gather work for him? Well why you going on vacation early? That school calendar's been set for about a year. Okay, you're gonna go see grandma. Grandma's not gonna be there during spring break? Okay, okay. Well, here, let me write a note: "Mr. Brown, Steven's mama called. She would like you to spend three or four hours gathering homework two weeks early, so he can go on vacation, and don't forget a reading log so she can sign it and act like her child read, even though he didn't."

Hello? Yeah, uh huh, is this April's mama? Yeah, she's not at school today. Oh, she's sick? Has she got a fever? No? Okay, is she throwing up? No? Okay. Why you think she's sick? She told you she was sick, and she needed to stay home. Okay, what's she doing right now, watching the TV and playing some video games? All right, well, I'm-a send the Easter Bunny over to your house later with her homework. Oh, you don't believe that? Well, you just seem to be somebody that's believing a lot of things they shouldn't be believing. I hope we see her tomorrow. All right, goodbye.

The office is the lifeline of the school. The school secretary serves as the liaison to everybody: students, parents, teachers, paraprofessionals, guests, and servicepeople. She needs to be reliable, happy, helpful, and a great first impression for anybody who calls or comes into the office.

However, that role is also one of the most stressful and low-paid jobs there is at a school. The school secretary has to deal with irate parents who call up, teachers who don't follow the rules, and upset kids who have been sent to the office because they're in trouble. That's why I made a video to say, "Gosh, it would be nice if the secretary was able to say what she really wants to a self-centered parent or an uncooperative teacher."

Of course, school secretaries don't get to speak that way, even though people talk to them any way they want to. One of the things that stresses me the most is when parents call in and are as rude as they can be to my secretaries, yet when they get to me, they're nice. My assistants take abuse, help solve problems, and talk parents down when they call in upset because they forgot to bring their child her special lunch, or they think their kid is the victim of bullying. "Oh my gosh," they say. "I'd be upset, too. I can't imagine that."

More parents need to remember that there are 725 kids in the school. You may have only one or two children, but we have hundreds of other children to deal with whose parents feel the same way about their kids as you do about yours. Don't berate my secretary because she put you on hold or didn't get back to you immediately. She most likely had three kids in front of her: one throwing up, one crying, and the other asking to use a phone, while there was another parent on the line and a father standing in front of her asking her on a date (yes, I'm serious). As a parent, you may think, "Why are you not getting me everything I need right now?" The answer is: there are most likely 16 other people she's dealing with.

Do you want good karma at your child's school? The next time you give a gift to your teacher, give one to the secretary. The next time you send a thankful email to the teacher, send one to the secretary as well. Behind every successful teacher or principal is a well-organized, pleasant, capable secretary who most likely doesn't get enough respect— even from the people she works with.

Teachers often have the same mentality parents have. You might deal with 30 kids, but she's dealing with 725 kids *and* the staff. I tell the teachers, "Don't tick off the cafeteria workers and don't tick off the secretaries." She's the direct line to the principal. She's the one who decides how quickly she'll pass notes along. She decides whether she wants to walk a delivery down to a classroom and be helpful. She can easily put every phone call that comes in to your classroom and interrupt your instruction every day, but she chooses not to.

Teachers should aspire to build relationships with the school secretary the way parents build relationships with them. Find out your school secretary's favorite treat and drop it by someday as a surprise. Be respectful. Remember your secretary on Assistant's Day and have the kids write thank you notes. Send appreciative emails: "You did a great job with that situation. Thank you for not sending that parent directly to my classroom and taking a note for me instead."

Also? Administrators? Do not make your school secretary do cafeteria duty. Do not. I'm floored when this happens. They already deal with enough stress. The secretary is the one who spends 30 minutes on the phone hearing about the grandfather who lost his toes to diabetes and why the family's got to go out of town even though Aunt Judy won't be very happy to see them. Don't make her clean up spilled chocolate milk off the floor on top of that.

There are so many people in a school system who don't get enough pay or respect, but the school secretaries are at the top of my list. They're kind of like the counselor to the entire school community. Stop reading right now and email yours to say "thanks." The next time you go to the store, pick up a candy bar and bring it in, because your school secretary needs it and deserves it.

20

THE SCHOOL NURSE
Administrating Band-Aids and Eyerolls

**An Average Five Minutes
in the Life of a School Nurse**

Hello? This is the school nurse. Is this Billy's mama? You're going to need to come get him. He's thrown up. What do you mean, "Again?" If he threw up three times this morning, why did you put him on the school bus? Oh, you got a hair appointment this afternoon? Well, I'm sorry, you're going to need to come get him. No, I cannot keep him until after your hair appointment. No. I can't just give him medicine. What do you mean you sent medicine in his pocket? Billy, you got some medicine in your pocket? What did you do with it? He gave it out on the school bus. Great. So now I got a sick drug dealer up in the school nurse office.

Hey, honey, what are you doing? No, I can't see nothing. I'm looking right at your . . . You mean that little teeny scratch right there? You don't need no Band-Aid for . . . You know what? Your teacher's got Band-Aids. Yes, she does. I gave her a big ole Ziploc baggie at the beginning of the school year, so I wouldn't have to deal with things like this. What do you mean? Oh, her desk is too

---

messy, she can't find them? Here, take this Band-Aid, and you go tell your teacher she needs to clean her desk.

Hey, honey, what's going on? You're not feeling good? You going to throw up? Well, what did you eat for breakfast? Four strawberry milks, two chocolate milks, two Pop Tarts and a chicken biscuit? You know what, honey? We're going to learn something today, it's called "natural consequences." Here, you take this trash can and you set it right next to your desk and you come back later and tell me what you learned today.

Hello, Miss Williams? This is the school nurse calling. Are you going to come up and get this medicine before you go on that field trip? Yes, you need to come get it. It's a brand-new thing we're doing. We've been doing it for about 17 years now.

Hi, honey. Your mama said to give that to me? Wait, it's a hair brush. What's going on? You got head lice? What are you doing at school? Your mama wants me to fix . . . What did she do last night about it? You say she just brushed your hair while you watched the Cinderella? No, you got to go home, you can't stay here with head lice. I don't care if she washed it with dishwashing liquid, you got to go home. Go sit right back there, I'm going to call your mama. Nope, a little farther, a little farther. Excellent.

Oh, hello, you must be Susie's mom. You sent some essential oils in with your child? You want me to rub it where? No, I ain't rubbing it on your child. No, I don't care if you do think it calms her down. You want to calm your child down? Quit giving her Pop-Tarts for breakfast. No, that essential oil ain't doing nothing but stinking up that classroom. Goodbye.

Hey, honey, what's going on? You got some Cocoa Puffs up both nostrils? No, I ain't got no tweezers. You go back to class. You tell your teacher to pinch real hard, and then you blow. Pinch and blow, pinch and blow. They'll just crumble right on out of there.

Hey, what are you doing up here? You don't feel good, you want to go home? Nope, I'm sorry you got to stay here. I'm sorry if you don't like it here. Nope, you got to stay. It don't make a difference that you don't got no friends, you got to stay. Because you're the principal. That's right, now get back to your office.

I made that video as a tribute to school nurses, who possess a level of professionalism and knowledge that nobody else in the school office has but who deal with so much. I've seen parents send a toothbrush to school with their child, saying to the nurse, "I can't get my child to brush her teeth in the morning. Will you brush them for her?" Parents have even sent their kids to school with suppositories and asked the nurse to insert them (nice try).

Here are the three biggest avoidable health issues that keep school nurses busier than they should be:

Diarrhea

We get parents all the time who say, "My child's got the backdoors," which is an old-fashioned saying from around here to refer to you-know-what. Parents need to be mindful of what position they put teachers and school nurses in when they send a young child to school who might be on the mend but still has bathroom issues. Say you're in the middle of a reading lesson, and a child with diarrhea announces she's got an upset stomach, but the policy is that you can't go to the bathroom more than once every 10 minutes. Well, if you've got an upset stomach, you can't necessarily hold it for 10 minutes. Also, younger students don't know what to do when they've gone to the bathroom and there's a mess. Parents know this as well as anyone, yet they sometimes seem to choose to forget it.

Fever

A struggle we have is when parents reason, "If I give my child Motrin, I'll get four hours out of her and pick her up after lunch if I have to." If your child's sick enough to need medicine, maybe she's just not ready to go back to school. We understand as parents you may need that time, but as a teacher, it's stressful to teach a child who might look okay but it's only because she got medicine, and now she's spreading sickness around everywhere.

Emotional Issues

Children can make themselves ill with worry, or think that if they act sick, they won't have to face issues like bullies or trouble at home. Unfortunately, adults can miss that for three or four days and suddenly realize, "Wait, she's not sick. She's upset about something that happened on the playground." Illness and behavior can go hand in hand—whenever a child's behavior changes, 90 percent of the time it's due to actual illness, but otherwise a kid who acts sick can very well be indicating another concern.

The types of parents who drive schools the craziest are the ones who keep their children home when they have a hangnail, as well as the ones who send their kids to school even after they've thrown up three times before they left the house.

When it comes to the first type of parent, schools can take action and crack down harder on truancy. A lot of parents don't take school attendance seriously—they'll keep kids home because they took a lot of Fridays off for three-day weekends and want to do something fun, or for a swim competition, or just because the parent stayed up too late. By the time their child is actually sick, they're arguing with the school because their kid has already had 15 absences while we roll our eyes wondering if this is just another day off.

What's trickier are the parents who send their kids to school sick because they can't afford to miss work. These children are at their desks at 7:35 a.m. with a temperature of 104 degrees, and of course three days later you've got 10 children out sick. It's understandable why parents do that, especially those who live from paycheck to paycheck. If they have to stay home with a child, that's eight hours of work, maybe $40, that they're not getting paid.

I wish I had a solution for those parents. It's an ongoing struggle. I remember when my wife and I had to invite friends over to help pull nits from our kids' hair because it was all hands on deck—all three children came down with lice at one point! With my short attention span, it was a killer to sit there sifting through my daughter's thick, dark hair looking for nits while she watched *Cinderella*.

It's stressful for parents when a student is sick and there are last-minute decisions to make about work and childcare. Aside from advocating for policy that's friendlier to working parents, administrators can help and give families a heads-up about the advent of the flu or strep throat at school, what to look for, and when to take a child to the doctor. Parents can help when they receive these materials by thinking, proactively, "Okay, so if Susie wakes up with strep this week, what can we do? Can we split up the day? Can grandma come help out?"—anything to lessen the last-minute panic of a sick kid on an important day of work.

Teachers can also help lessen the workload of the school nurse. I'm talking about the ones who send students up for a Band-Aid because a kid got a paper cut in the middle of a math lesson, or a kid's tooth is loose. The nurse thinks, *What in the world do you want me to do with this loose tooth? Whatever you thought I could do, you could've done in the classroom.* The teacher is thinking, meanwhile, *It sure is easy to send this kid to the school nurse, who has nothing else going on.*

And that's absolutely not the truth. Incidentally, a school nurse would never call down to a teacher and say, "I don't think that your vocabulary words are appropriate for your grade level," but a teacher will override a school nurse to call a parent and say, "You need to come get your child," even though the school nurse has said he's okay. Then the parent shows up at the school office and says, "My child's sick, I was told to come and get him," and the school nurse is going, "Wait, I didn't say that." Many teachers need to get out of their own box and respect the school nurse's polices and requests.

Do you know who I love? I love parents who come up to the office and say, "Listen, my kid's gonna try and call me today. He's gonna act like he's sick. I've taken his temperature. He is not sick. He's trying to get out of his math test. There is not a reason why he shouldn't be at school. He does not need to call me unless there's a real emergency. Otherwise I'll see you at 2:30." Those kids always look at us like, "Okay, I've been had."

I want to say it again: I love those parents.

21

PROFESSIONAL DEVELOPMENT

Teaching Teachers for as Long as Their Attention Spans Will Allow

Principal-to-Principal Tip

I would like to share some things with my fellow principals that I'm sure will get me in trouble with all the teachers, but I would like to tell you about what's really going on in your staff meetings.

First of all, if you see a teacher come in with a fancy notebook, and she's taking notes over your riveting discussion, and you turn around and the teacher next to her has the same notebook, and she's fervently taking notes on your riveting conversation, be aware: your conversation is not riveting, and no one is taking notes on it. They're passing notes like you used to do in high school. They're talking about what's happening on the Kurdashians or on *Real Housewives*, not about what you're talking about.

Next, you need to be aware of the T T T. That's the Texting under The Table. Teachers have figured this out in several different ways. First, they rub their heads like they have a headache so that you will feel sorry for them, but what they're doing is looking down at their other hand, which is under the table, texting. It's a trick.

Now, you have some very intelligent teachers who have set this up from the beginning of the year because for the first month of school, they paid attention to everything, and they nodded their head at you like they were right with you. They're setting up the T T T. For the rest of the year, whenever you say something that's a little sad like, "We're almost at the end of our allotted copies for this month, so you can't make any more," they will look down and shake their head. You think they're just reacting to the sad thing you just said, but really, they are T T T ing.

Last, if you host your staff meeting in the computer lab because you're teaching some newfangled technology that you want them to implement tomorrow, and every time you step toward the computers you hear, "click, click, click, click, click, click, click, click, click, click," it's not because the teachers are using the technology you're teaching. It's because they are on Groupon, and they think you're going to step down the aisles and see that they're not paying attention to you. So, if you're in the computer lab, and you keep hearing "click, click, click, click, click" every time you take one step toward the computers, it's because your teachers are getting amazing deals, not paying attention to you.

As I write, I'm on my way to our districtwide leadership professional development, which spans three days over the summer.

The first day is fantastic. I love reuniting with all my colleagues. We socialize and enjoy great sessions on topics like curriculum, time management, or how to build relationships with peers.

On the second day, I start to drag a bit, but the conference provides breakfast, so it's still a fun time of fellowship. The classes feel a bit longer, and just like an elementary school student watching the clock near dismissal, I keep an eye on the clock for the last hour to make sure that I can head out before the traffic starts to get heavy.

The third day is slow. I tend to come in right at starting time and pull my computer out in case I get bored. In no time, I'm cruising Pinterest or Teachers Pay Teachers and am already thinking about what I'll do when I get home from the conference.

Unfortunately, this third-day mentality is the only setting teachers have during professional development—and for good reason.

As an administrator, I think carefully about how to best do professional development with my staff: I want to be effective, but realistic about how much time and attention teachers can give me. I can't sit through a six-hour training, so how in the world can I ask someone else to do the same? When I do plan in-service days, I try to include ways to make the most out of professional development but also support positive climate and culture, including:

- **Starting right on time.** When I stroll in late, I send the message that I think my time is more valuable than the teachers'.

- **Making time for some type of group activity or socialization at the beginning,** like a little game or even just conversation, to start everyone off on a friendly and congenial note.

- **Including 15-minute breaks every 50 minutes.**

- **Asking teachers to put their cell phones away during training time.** I'm not a huge stickler about this, though. I have children and stress in my life just like anyone, so if I need to send a text or answer the phone, then I do it. I trust that my staff members are doing the same and I generally don't have a problem with that, although once in a while I will have one staff member who seems to be on the phone the entire time and we have a private discussion.

- **Giving an extended lunch of about 90 minutes**, so staff has time to go somewhere, eat, relax, and then get back to professional development without rushing. Longer, relaxed lunches are a great opportunity for teams to get to know one another rather than a 45-minute dash. This also gives teachers more time to complete work that they might be concerned about.

- **Allowing teachers to have time at the end of a professional development** to meet with their colleagues and discuss what they've learned.

- **Ending early if possible.** A six-hour professional development that starts exactly on time and all the way to the end is stressful for me, so I try to make sure we leave about 15 minutes early.

- **Lightening up.** I think a major part of school culture is a good running joke. For instance, my staff teases me over how I can never stay on topic, or how I can never remember the correct names of anything, and I'm fine with that. I believe in the value of a quick break for something funny and silly. It's valuable to remember that if our kids need that, it's probably good for grownups, too. There's always room for jokes during professional development, and administrators can set that tone.

- **Playing favorites.** I got this advice from Ron Clark, a popular motivational speaker and educator. In his talks, he says that teachers accuse him of having favorite staff members. His response to them is, "Yes, I do." Play favorites with people who stay until 5:30 p.m. Play favorites with teachers who go to professional development and implement what they learn in their classrooms. If you spend $1,000 on a professional conference where attendees stay three nights in a hotel someplace appealing, make sure you send staff members who are hard-working, respected, and eager to share what they learn. When you send a leader to a professional development session, that money is well-spent because that thousand dollars ends up affecting their entire team, like my teacher who showed us what she learned about sentence frames for foreign language immersion classes. Play favorites, and don't let anyone make you feel guilty about it. If they give you a hard time, just tell them Ron Clark told you it was OK.

I am realistic—I know professional development or in-service days can often be tedious or overwhelming. When teachers aren't engaged, sometimes the behavior they display in meetings is the same behavior that irritates us in the classroom, like texting under the table or passing notes.

Teachers and administrators should strive to focus on one or two things that clicked from professional development, that made them say, "Oh, I needed to be reminded of that," or, "That's something I hadn't thought of." I know not all teachers will walk away with tremendous insights from every training session, but even during the world's longest six-hour meeting, it's still good to hold onto the idea that there's something small you can use to improve your classroom instruction.

If you're a teacher or administrator and you go to professional development with your colleagues, you should aim not only to learn with them, but also to have fun with them. If you're going with a team, be a team. Meet up for one meal or sit together during one discussion. If you're going with someone you don't know, get to know them.

Professional development should also be a rejuvenation of yourself, to say, "I have this conference until 4 p.m., and from 4 to 10 p.m. is my time, and I'm going to go eat out, and I'm going to relax. I'm going to go back to the room, have a treat from the vending machine, and stay up and watch movies." Before I started traveling so much for my events, the reward for me when attending a training was taking hour-long baths and reading a *People* magazine without one of my kids interrupting me. Training should be a refresher, not just for you professionally and in-structionally, but also for your mental health.

PART **6**

NOTES HOME
Strengthening the
Parent/Teacher Connection

22

A TWO-WAY STREET

How Parents and Teachers Can Better
Communicate on an Ongoing Basis

Clear, pleasant, regular communication *can* happen between parents and teachers, if they both recognize opportunities to better support each other. Otherwise, you end up with a teacher having this kind of exchange over the phone, day after day:

Is this Billy's mom? Hi there, I'm sorry to call you during the day. Oh, I'm sorry that it's your nap time, but I just thought you'd want to know that Billy used some inappropriate language in the lunch line today. He said he didn't want no dang fries on his tray, but he used the other D word. Yeah, that's the one.

So I just felt like you'd want to know. No, there wasn't pizza today. So, okay, you're saying he might be mad that there was no pizza, but that doesn't mean he should be using that kind of language in the lunchroom. Well, I don't know where Suzy was standing. What's that got to do with anything? I don't know whether Suzy whispered to him to say it or not, but even if she did, he shouldn't have been using that language. Don't you agree? Well, no, I can't make sure that he's not in line with Suzy anymore. It's not got anything to do with Suzy, it has to do with Billy using the D word in the lunch line.

You're saying he's still mad at his teacher from Halloween? That was like two weeks ago. It was not her rule that he couldn't wear a vampire costume. It was the school rule. You can't wear scary costumes to Halloween. Well, just because he's still mad about the vampire costume, don't mean he can use bad language in the lunchroom. No, you don't need to send Grandma up here to yell at him for you. Grandma don't need to come set nobody straight. I'm just calling to tell you that he said a bad word in the lunchroom line. I'm not sure what it his grandma's going to do up here. I'm just going to tell her the same thing: "Hey, Grandma, he said the D word in the lunchroom line."

Well, I'm sorry, I don't know who beeped at you this morning in the car rider line. There're 725 kids here, so I don't know whose parent drives a big pickup truck that may have beeped at you, and why that would make Billy say the D word.

Okay, look, I'm just calling to tell you that he used the D word in the lunchroom line, and I'd like you to talk to him about it tonight. Well, I'd like you to say, "Don't use those words at school." No, I'm sure it's not the teacher that he heard it from. You know, how about this? How about if we just deal with this here, and you go back to your dang nap. Sounds good.

But it doesn't have to be this way. Both parents and teachers, with just a little bit of communication, compassion, and compromise (remember, from the introduction to this book?) can improve how they relay information to each other in the interest of students.

How Parents Can Better Communicate with Teachers

Pass along Good News

When your child comes home excited about something from school, tell the teacher. "Today at dinner, Billy couldn't stop talking about how Susie brought in the worms for show and tell." Just a simple note like that makes a teacher's day.

Give the Teacher the Benefit of the Doubt

Many parents say, "My child would never lie," or "I know my child lies, but he's not lying now." I have literally never met a child who would not stretch the truth or omit a detail if he thought it was gonna get him out of trouble. I once had a knock-down drag-out with a parent because her child brought high-heeled shoes to school. The parent swore up and down that the teacher who reported it must be the liar. The whole situation was humorous to me—you would trust a six-year-old over a professional adult? Of course, the mother ended up coming in and the child pulled, guess what, high-heeled shoes out of her backpack.

To better support your teacher, first talk to your child. Don't rely on a child to relay information. Rather than fire off a five-page email, try, "Billy said that he got pushed down on the playground today. Can you give me any insight?" Billy may have omitted the part where he called the other kids names.

Don't Put Down the Teacher in Front of Your Kids

We'll have kids who come here and say, "My mommy said you're just being mean," or "My dad said that I don't need to believe that." If you want to badmouth the teacher to your spouse or to your own mom, that's fine, but don't do it while the kids are around unless you want us to call you.

Don't Go above the Teacher's Head

Parents, understand that teachers and administrators butt heads and have workplace drama like any teams do. And there is something you can do, the next time you have a concern about your child's teacher:

Go directly to the teacher. Do NOT go see the principal.

It makes teachers livid when parents go above them to me, and I don't like it either. It's disrespectful to the teacher. The parents are basically saying, "I have a concern because I have listened exclusively to my child and rather than discuss it with the teacher I would like you to step in and fix it."

I have a script now for any time parents try to go over the teacher's head, whether they complain about too much homework, not enough homework, or that they want their child moved away from another child:

"Before you say anything, have you contacted Ms. Jones, and does she know that you went to me?"

If it's "yes," then I can get involved, but sometimes parents will say, "Well, we want your opinion first before we go to Ms. Jones."

My response: "That's disrespectful to Ms. Jones, and it's also disrespectful to me as a principal, because you want me to listen to only your side, which isn't fair to my staff."

Think of it this way: how do you feel when your children resolve conflict on their own versus coming to you to complain about a million different incidents you didn't see that have nothing to do with you? It makes life easier for your principal, and thus the entire school, if you and your teachers can resolve issues on your own.

Go Through Your Child's Bag
When He Comes Home

It's frustrating for teachers when a parent calls and says, "I didn't know about this field trip," and you think, "Well, we've passed out four different pieces of information." Then you go to the child's bag and find 15 days' worth of newsletters, notes, and homework. Teachers get that life happens—the occasional forgotten form or theme day is understandable—but when it happens a lot, there are consequences and unfortunately, they will eventually affect your child who has to discover that he can't participate in PE when he has flip-flops on.

I know that in the rush of coming home, doing homework, making dinner, and getting through bedtime it can be easy to forget checking your child's bag, but work toward making it an automatic habit, like dropping your keys in the same place every day when you come home. Find a routine that works for you, whether it's reviewing your child's bag right before dinnertime, before teeth-brushing, or even on the ride home. Consistency is key.

Speak Gently

Sometimes the teacher doesn't communicate well, but a parent can counter this in a peaceful way with the words they choose.

Instead of: "You said you would send home weekly newsletters—are you ever going to get around to that?"

Try: "I'm not receiving communications from you. Are you sending something that I'm not getting?"

How Teachers Can Better Communicate with Parents

Send Out a Communication Time Frame During the First Week of School

Teachers have to step up and say, "I communicate in one of these three ways: a phone call, a text message, or an email within 24 hours. Please do follow up if you haven't heard from me in 24 hours." Then they need to absolutely stick with it. That will help address the issue of the parent who says, "I sent you a note this morning and it's now 5:00 p.m.—why have you not called me back?"

Have Compassion for Parents

Particularly when it comes to low-income or other struggling families, teachers should take a moment to reflect on their students' home life. Some parents who work two jobs and barely get by might take it as a personal attack if a teacher calls with bad news and relays the information in a way that sounds like the parent is at fault.

Don't get me wrong; there have been times when we've said, "We'll have to deal with this behavior issue at school 'cause we get no support from this child's parent, who always gives us either an excuse or an argument. From 7:15 a.m. to 2:45 p.m. we will deal with this at school in the best way we can." But most of the time, when parents and teachers can throw each other some extra empathy, patience, and helpful information, it can help strengthen not just your child but the entire class.

23

PARENT-TEACHER CONFERENCES
Some Basic Rules

A Teacher's Guide to What You Want to Say at Parent-Teacher Conferences Versus What You Will Actually Say

PARENT: We think Billy is gifted. Can we get him tested for the gifted and talented program?

WHAT YOU WANT TO SAY: Billy, gifted? He is gifted all right. You know what he's gifted at? Losing his lunchbox every single day. Regularly coming to school with his shoes on the wrong feet. He's also really gifted at bumping into the wall when he walks down the hallway.

WHAT YOU WILL SAY: Billy is special in many ways. We can certainly look into that.

* * *

PARENT: We don't have any behavior issues at home with Billy. Maybe you're not challenging him. Maybe he's bored in your classroom and if you challenged him he would be better behaved.

WHAT YOU WANT TO SAY: His behavior is because he's bored? You know what I saw yesterday after school? Him kicking and screaming at you because you forgot to put a Go-Gurt in his lunch. Do you know what his behavior issues are? You let him get away with whatever he wants to at home and then he comes to school and thinks he can do the same thing. You want his behavior to improve? It don't have nothing to do with being challenged. Maybe you should work on his bad behavior at home. What do you think?

WHAT YOU WILL SAY: I've never made that observation. I appreciate you bringing it to my attention.

Parent-teacher conferences are excellent opportunities to discuss a child's progress, but they don't always go the way you want them to. Here are some basic rules for parents on how to make the most of yours:

Show up on time. You wouldn't believe how many parents are no-shows and then reschedule and reschedule. This isn't helpful for children, and it's just plain disrespectful to teachers.

Don't disrespect the teacher during the meeting. Some parents are angry about an issue and come in hot, which can escalate the situation. If you can't handle being in the room with the teacher without shouting, contact the principal.

If you're not on good terms with your child's other parent, leave it at the door. When the teacher says, "He doesn't turn his homework in consistently," I've seen parents argue, "Well, he's always got his homework when he is with me." Or, "He leaves my house with the homework, so I don't what you're doing that you can't get his homework in." Don't drag teachers into that. You chose to have a child with the person in the conference with you—buck up and act like an adult.

Stay in the present. This is not the time to delve into an issue from three months ago or to badmouth your child's teacher from last year.

Come in with an idea of what you want to discuss. If you're concerned about your child's reading progression, his relationship with his best friend, or the amount of homework he gets, these types of conversations are best held face to face. So much can be lost in the context of email or even report cards.

Don't take it too hard. It can be easy for involved/perfectionist parents to focus on any negatives they hear about their child, but they need to remember the common goal of improvement. Every child needs to improve at something.

Respect time limits. If you need additional time with your teacher, he or she will be happy to make another appointment, but remember that other parents are waiting their turn, and, also, as hard as it can be to believe, your teacher actually needs to go home at some point.

Administrators can also help teachers during parent-teacher conferences by setting a schedule. One of the best things we ever did was allot 20 minutes for every parent-teacher conference. We start at 4 p.m., ring one bell at 4:15, and then ring another at 4:20. The 4:15 bell means "Time to wrap it up" and the 4:20 bell indicates you need to start the next conference. This keeps parents on task. Also, place chairs outside the classroom so parents can wait right there and not wander off. The schedule keeps the evening from running late and also helps illuminate when parents are late because you can say, "I'm sorry, but we have a set schedule and you missed your time. We will have to reschedule."

24

REPORT CARDS
Only Part of the Bigger Picture

Teacher Translate:
The Ultimate Report Card Helper!

I'm extremely excited to announce a new app I have developed just for teachers. It's like Google Translate, where you say something in English and it translates it back into Germanish or something like that. Teacher Translate interprets comments when you're struggling with what to say on a report card.

You say: "Your child keeps licking a bunch of other kids out on the playground. What's that all about?"
Teacher Translate: "Your child has a unique way of making friends."

You say: "Billy ain't paying no attention in class. He's not getting any of the things I'm trying to teach because he's too busy looking all around."
Teacher Translate: "Billy's curiosity about the things going on around him often obstructs his ability to grasp certain concepts."

You say: Your child is a bully, and no one wants to play with
her because she is mean as a snake.
Teacher Translate: Social skills are an area we will be
focusing on this year.

Teachers and paraprofessionals can ruin a relationship with a parent
with a single poorly chosen comment. One of the most important
things we can do as educators is to spend time making sure the feedback we write in planners and especially on report cards is worded positively. Report cards end up being primary sources for growing families.
Parents pull out their old report cards and read them to their children,
which leads to a great discussion about what type of student their parent was. I can still remember comments on my report cards, specifically
one from third grade: "Gerry wants to be in charge at all times, and
often that gets him into trouble." I still have that report card, even at
51 years old. It makes me laugh.

This is why I made the Teacher Translate video. Teachers need to
recognize that children's report cards are a type of family record—like a
birth certificate or a diploma—that gets put on the refrigerator, placed
in a keepsake box, and taken out and looked at for decades. Therefore,
I personally advise teachers to think twice before they put anything
tremendously negative on a child's report card.

Of course, that's not to say that teachers shouldn't impart negative
or constructive comments when necessary, but the heaviest and most
detailed of these should be saved for emails, phone calls, and meetings.
Report cards should be a record of the positive aspects of a student's
year, which, let's face it, means that report cards don't often show the
whole story.

This is one of the reasons parents should look at report cards as just
one piece of a bigger picture of their child's education. Another reason
is that grading systems can vary from teacher to teacher, especially in

primary grades where they get S+ and smiley faces. And all of a sudden, a child is getting a C in third grade, but the teacher really doesn't want the child to get a C, so she starts to build certain things into grades like class participation. By fourth grade, the child gets a teacher who doesn't believe in putting class participation into a grade. So, suddenly, parents who thought they had a B student actually have a C student.

If parents are on top of the day-to-day work that comes home in their children's backpacks and online parent portals—and their essays and syllabuses in high school—if they have a rough idea of what percentages go into a report card, there shouldn't be any major surprises on their children's report cards.

If you're a teacher, your best practice is to communicate to parents, "This is what we've been working on. This is how you can check on your child's work." If a straight A student is suddenly receiving a B, the teacher owes the parent a heads-up: "Hey, I just want to let you know that your child's work lately has been three days late, and it will affect his grade." This is not a requirement, but if you're a teacher who says, "It's not my responsibility to let parents know about bad grades," don't act surprised when you have an angry parent. Be proactive.

Of course, teachers shouldn't have to babysit parents, provide daily updates on their kids, or make a call every time a child misses an assignment (particularly once they're in late middle school and high school). Students will never be completely reliable when it comes to reporting how they're doing with their work, so parents need to meet teachers halfway, look at their kids' notebooks, and check in on parent portals.

A parent will sometimes come in to yell about his child's report card and demand that a grade gets changed. That's always a ton of fun. Trust me, a teacher doesn't want a parent to be surprised by a report card. A surprised parent is a ticked-off parent.

PART 7

EXTRACURRICULARS
Fun at School

25

SPORTS
They're Great (but Not *That* Great)

I was heavily involved in sports when I was a high school student in Florida: tennis team, diving team, swim team. For two hours in the morning, we'd practice at the local pool, go to school, come back, and practice for two more hours in the afternoon. My friends, family, and I also could usually be spotted in the stands at school football and basketball games. My best friends were high-achieving swimmers who received full scholarships to high-end Division One schools because of their abilities.

And look at me now! As you can see, I'm a famous professional athlete, making millions of dollars each year in endorsements.

Seriously, when I was a kid, sports were just a fun activity to do with friends, to keep me healthy and out of trouble. However, as wonderful as athletics can be, when you let your child's sport take over your life and the self-esteem of your kid, then you can come into some huge struggles.

At one of my former schools, there was one parent who would get overly intense at basketball games, screaming at his own child. I didn't want to address it right there in front of everybody, but one day I called him and said, gently, "I don't know if you realized how harsh you sound—it's not the yelling, but it's that you don't say anything positive, and it affects everyone who can hear you." Thankfully, he was receptive to it.

But some parents don't want to hear this, especially those who have invested a lot of time and money into athletics. Here's the hard truth: for the majority of children, sports are not the start of some lifelong success story, and their importance in many children's lives is overinflated. Odds are, your child won't get a full ride and become a professional athlete. When it comes to student athletes, "student" comes first. Plus, sports aren't the only healthy way for your child to socialize. Your child can also build relationships through Scouts, drama, church, or world travel—all experiences that will stick with your child beyond college. When you put too many eggs in one basket, the eggs can break. It's a difficult time if your child didn't make the travel team but all his friends did, and you've based his entire life on soccer or baseball. Plus, do you want your child to question your love for him if football is the only thing you have bonded over when suddenly he can't play?

Last year I had a parent call me, angry because she got a truancy letter when her daughter missed too many school days for sports. "She will be an Olympian, and we feel she should be excused," the mom said. Well, your child may be an Olympian someday, but for now she's in fourth grade and doesn't need to miss three days of school every week.

There's a happy medium. Three days per year? That's not a big deal. Once a week? That hurts your child's academics over the long term. If you want to pull your child out of school and get a private tutor or homeschool her because you're convinced she will be a famous dancer on TV someday, that's your decision, but if your child is enrolled in a traditional school, then you need to respect the traditional school calendar and the traditional school day. Boom.

There are many benefits to organized sports: they build relationships, teach sportsmanship, and help kids learn strategy and perseverance. Thus, sometimes parents wonder how long to keep a kid on a team when the child complains about not having fun. Is it better to just let a child do what he wants or do you model sticking with something and not being a quitter?

I think you should want your child to follow through, and not necessarily drop a sport in the middle of the season, but also explore why your child feels that way. I don't go by the philosophy of, "You will never, ever quit because we signed up for this team and you're going to stick it out" when the coach is not nice, the child doesn't have any friends on the team, people are using bad language, and the athlete never feels successful. Your child can learn valuable life lessons through many venues other than sports.

When I was in high school, we had a star student who was ineligible to wrestle because of his grades. The principal overrode it because the student was such a good wrestler and the team needed him. This move backfired on the principal. I think he believed that everyone at school would be mad at him if he didn't let this high-level athlete compete in the match, but the response from parents and the community was, "What do you mean? There are rules here."

I do think principals can help take the pressure off team sports to emphasize the successes of all school organizations and not raise athletics above all else. Sports are just one way schools can experience pride; there's also the chess team, the debate team, the school band, and the work of volunteer groups. There's room for all students to celebrate victories, not just the athletes.

26

HOLIDAY PARTIES
It's the Most Exhausting Time of the Year

At a lot of schools, holiday parties have been cut way down from what they used to be because districts don't want to offend people who might have issues with Christmas or Halloween or whatever. However, even if classes have only a Valentine's Day party and an end-of-year party, that doesn't mean that there isn't still plenty of school party drama, which, like most drama, is avoidable.

It's not about the activities, snacks, or theme. What really makes for a good party is teacher personality. I have a teacher who's a great friend of mine whom I tease all the time 'cause her parties are five Cheetos, three Skittles, and a juice box. She just wants her parties to be relaxation time for the kids. "We're not going to work," she says. "We will watch a video clip, play a couple of games, and then we'll eat." Then you've got the teacher down the hall who has tables set up with food and then she has to figure out what to do with all the snacks that went uneaten. Guess what? Both classes had a good time at their parties because it was different than their everyday schedule.

Teachers primarily want to make sure that parties aren't chaotic, but then you have parents who want the kindergarteners to do a 16-stage craft where they paint snowmen with their thumbs and all of a sudden, you've got 25 kindergartners with white paint on them. Or there are the parents who say, "We'll rent bouncy houses and have pizza delivered and the firemen will come over and squirt all the kids," when the teacher just wanted to do some outdoor games, have time on the playground, eat some popsicles, and call it a day.

Parents often don't consider the importance of school equity when it comes to parties. Otherwise, you've got one grade level that has a pancake breakfast with a clown delivering balloons and another across the hallway with just powdered donuts and milk. These types of discrepancies are an especially big deal when families have more than one child at the school.

When it comes to parties, teachers can do their part to minimize drama and effectively communicate details about class parties to parents—what time it is, what kids need to bring, and whether parents are allowed—because otherwise the school office is taking calls about the party all day.

Class parties are like any part of school where communication is clear and effective—teachers need to give parents all the information, parents need to be clear with teachers about any ideas they have, and there should be a general consensus that the teacher knows best when it comes to what constitutes a good party.

Because the bottom line is, if the kids aren't working, it's a party to them.

VALENTINES FOR PRINCIPALS TO GIVE THEIR TEACHERS THIS FEBRUARY 14

FRONT: I like you more than a snow day.

INSIDE: Not really, but I do like you more than a staff meeting.

* * *

FRONT: Happy Valentine's Day! I like you more than a Goodie Table at Christmas.

INSIDE: Unless the Goodie Table had some of that derlicious buffalo chicken dip. Then you'd be a close second. But that's still good, don't you think?

* * *

FRONT: Happy Valentine's Day to my 13th favorite teacher.

INSIDE: You'd probably be in the top 10 if you weren't late all the time.

27

GIFTS

Never Necessary, Always Appreciated

Teacher Tip:
Get Your Principal What He
Really Wants This Holiday Season!

All you teachers reading right now undoubtedly lose sleep every year agonizing over the perfect holiday gift to get the principal in your life. Good news: I've created the ultimate coupon book to give principals, full of gift cards for the experiences they really want, including:

Shut It. Principals love this coupon for situations like when teachers come into the office complaining about the copier or their room being too hot. The principal can just slide you a "Shut It" coupon and you have to stop talking right then and there.

The Grim Reaper. This coupon lets teachers, instead of principals, be the deliverer of bad news. Like during pink slip time, your principal can give a teacher a "Grim Reaper" coupon, and

---

that teacher has to deliver the pink slips to everyone while the principal goes out and sees a movie.

No Crying. Principals don't know what to do when teachers cry, so this coupon is ideal for when a teacher lets the tears flow for whatever reason. Instead of offering a stiff professional hug or some unhelpful advice, the principal can just hand over this coupon and the teacher has to stop crying, no matter what.

Tell It Like It Is. If your principal gives you this coupon, you have to go tell it like it is to one of your colleagues. Like when a colleague brings a strawberry summer salad to Goodie Table Day, your principal can give you a "Tell It Like It Is" coupon, and you get to go to that colleague and tell her not to bring no strawberry summer salad to Goodie Table Day.

Rather than spend your hard-earned money on a gift, spend your weekend making some coupon books* for your principal. He will love it.

* * *

Principal Tip:
Get Your Teacher What She Really
Wants This Holiday Season!

I am now expanding my coupon book business and am offering coupons for principals to give teachers that they will love.

Get on out My Room. That's for when you come into the teacher's room, and they don't want you in there for one reason or

---

* No, that is not a typo—I said "books."

another, they can give you a "Get on out My Room" coupon, no questions asked.

How About If *You* Do It. When you're emailing teachers questions like "When you going to change your work in the hallway?" or "When you going to change your Christmas bulletin board? It's May," the teacher can give you a coupon that reads, "How about if you do it?" because that's what she really wants to say to you.

Roll on out the Bed. This is for when your teachers have had a bad night, and they just want to roll on out the bed and come into school in their Winnie the Pooh pajama T-shirt and a pair of jeans.

Switcharoonie. When a teacher gives you a "Switcharoonie," you gots to switcharoonie a bad kid out of their room with a good kid from another room.

Talk to the Hand. That's a general coupon a teacher can give the principal for when he's saying something dumb.

Sit, Smile, Listen, and Nod. When teachers come into your office, they can give you this coupon and you just have to sit, smile, listen, and nod no matter what they're saying. You can't get on your computer and try typing or acting like you're taking a fake phone call, either. You just have to sit, listen, smile, and nod.

Tell It Like It Is. This is a coupon a teacher can give the principal, and you have to go down and tell their colleagues exactly what that teacher's thinking. But you have to act like it's coming from you. So, if your teacher gives you a "Tell It Like It Is" coupon, you might have to go to another teacher and say, "That dress you're wearing today is hideous. Maybe you shouldn't wear it to school again. That's my opinion." Teachers would love that.

* * *

I promise you that giving out these coupon books will make you the most popular person in school. Happy holidays!

A teacher once told me that she got a thank you note from a parent, along with an Amazon gift card. She was so touched by the note that she almost wanted to tell the parent the gift card wasn't even necessary (but she didn't want to seem rude, of course).

Here's the bottom line: teachers like being appreciated, no matter the gift. Even if it's just a candy bar, it's the effort behind the gift that matters. But while gifts are a nice surprise, parents shouldn't feel obligated, especially if it's a financial burden.

But if you parents are inclined and have the means to give, here are a few presents teachers always seem to appreciate:

Amazon gift cards, Walmart gift cards, Target gift cards—because we don't make a lot of money. It's always a great gift to help relieve teachers from financial burden.

A gift card to Starbucks, Chili's, Applebee's, or another local restaurant—for when you want to give a teacher a gift to spend on themselves and not on the classroom.*

---

*But make sure a teacher drinks coffee before you give him a Starbucks card, or that your teacher drinks before giving her a bottle of wine. Just sayin'.

A package of stickers—because teachers spend their own money on that stuff.

A package of note cards—because most teachers will otherwise spend their own money on thank-you cards.

A donation to the school holiday fund (if there is one)—that way people like the PE, art, and science lab teachers as well as custodians don't get forgotten.

A heartfelt letter. It truly means a lot when you tell a teacher about how excited your child was for a lesson or when they came home talking about something in the classroom.

One of our traditions at Liberty Elementary is to offer parents the chance to send a wrapped "white elephant" gift, so that each staffer gets one at our holiday appreciation party. We have no idea what it is or who it's from. Parents send in a coffee mug, gift cards, T-shirt, or a pair of socks as a show of thanks. It's always fun to have something to open.

At Liberty, we also send teachers a survey of what they like, candy-wise, drink-wise, and salty chips–wise, so throughout the year we're able to access that valuable information and say, "Mrs. Smith loves Doritos and Diet Coke," which is great for rough days and as holiday gifts. (For the record, I prefer Zebra Cakes, Circus Peanuts, Swedish Fish, Easter Peeps, and basically anything that nobody else likes.)

I reiterate, parents shouldn't feel pressured to give at holiday time. My own kids were raised in a double-educator home, so my wife and I were mindful of our budget at Christmas when our children were in school. It can be a burden to say, "I'm going give the teachers $15 each." That's $45, which can be a whole lot to people.

When in doubt, a card that reads, "Thank you for everything you do" means a lot, even without a gift card inside.

28

GOODIE TABLE DAY
Christmas for the Principal

Do you remember Christmas as a child? It's such a thrilling time in the life of a young person. I remember getting so excited weeks ahead of time, wondering what kind of gifts I would get, mulling over what gifts I would bring to our family gatherings, guessing which relative would give me a gift that was needed but not really wanted (like underwear or socks), not being able to sleep on Christmas Eve, and waking up early to revel in the excitement.

Christmas was a magical season. As adults we often lose that feeling. But not me. I get that same feeling, but on Goodie Table Day.

What is Goodie Table Day, you ask? Gather 'round and let me tell you. Once a month, our staff gets together and bring treats from home, like a big family reunion, to celebrate teacher birthdays. And it makes me feel exactly the same way as I did at Christmas: building up excitement for weeks beforehand, wondering who's going to bring something great, thinking about what I'm going to bring to the table (usually drinks), and guessing who's going to bring the items that are much needed but not wanted (like a strawberry summer salad). I can't sleep the night before and I wake up early to revel in the excitement.

It's such a magical time.

The way it works is that we choose staff groups to bring in food each month. Usually it's one grade level plus one other area of the school, like special-area teachers, special education teachers, or the office staff. That way we have about 12 to 14 people hosting each Goodie Table Day. Most of the time it's lunch or breakfast, but sometimes it's snacks and desserts. No matter what it looks like, it's good to gather together and do something fun.

I especially like Goodie Table Day because it helps me work on my strategizing skills. I want to use my time wisely but also not get caught at the Goodie Table six times throughout the day. I usually start off at 10:30 a.m. with my third-grade teachers who go in the morning, because if they don't get their food and there's nothing left then they're grumpy all day. So, I start off there at 10:30 and stay for about 25 minutes.

I have to take a 15-minute break to let that first group leave the room and to allow a new group of people in, so no one knows I've been in there a second time. I go in at about 11:20 a.m. and I'm able to eat with the first and fifth grades. And then, of course, I repeat the process every 20 minutes in between a 25-minute lunch break so that the room clears out and everybody thinks I'm coming to the Goodie Table for the first time. It's such a wonderful part of my life.

There have been so many memorable goodies to look back on. I particularly enjoy how Goodie Table Day is often a day of appetizers. I love meatballs, little hot dogs, and buffalo dip. At my old school I had two secretaries, Miss Fadden and Miss Nancy, who made amazing desserts—I will never forget their strawberry cake, lemon cake, and date balls. But my favorite part of Goodie Table day is to see what teachers and staffers make at home, so I can try food I normally wouldn't.

We are tremendously blessed at Liberty to have one particular staff member who loves parties. She goes to the Dollar Tree and Home Goods to provide decorations for Goodie Table Day. In April we get Easter decorations; in May we have a summer-themed day; in October the room is decorated in orange and black. This isn't mandatory, but the decorations make Goodie Table Day even more special.

Honestly, what I like most about Goodie Table Day is watching groups of people who don't normally eat together sit and socialize. We often gather in our own teams to eat lunch and sometimes people aren't able or don't desire to do that because that's time they can get work done. But not on Goodie Table Day. On Goodie Table day all groups come together and intermingle. It's a great social time and a good way to build school morale.

If you've not done a Goodie Table Day at your school, I highly recommend you try one. Start out small, maybe with one at the start of the year, one at Christmas, and one at the end of the year. If you involve the entire staff, you have a ton of food and it defrays the cost.

These are just some initial Goodie Table Day suggestions. I have many more, but maybe I'll save them for my next book. This is a huge part of my school life and I've put a lot of thought into it. A successful Goodie Table Day makes a successful month, and, seriously, a happy group of teachers. Happy teachers, happy kids, happy parents.

So, to sum up, here's why Goodie Table Day is great:

- It's something to look forward to.
- It helps bring the school community together.
- Goodies.

PART 8

CODE OF CONDUCT—
FOR GROWNUPS

29

WHEN TEACHERS ARE OFF THE CLOCK
Somebody's Always Watching

Running into teachers outside of school can be a thrill for children, but tricky for the adults. At my last job in a small town, I dreaded trips to Walmart because in every aisle, I passed somebody that I knew who might look in my cart and notice that I had 14 boxes of Zebra Cakes and three varieties of cookies in there.

Teachers aren't like pop stars or professional athletes, but the bottom line is, if you're instructional, you're still something of a public figure—and that applies to bus drivers, paraprofessionals, cafeteria workers, and librarians as well. What we do in our own lives should be our own business. But if you're at Applebee's with 14 sorority sisters and the table is full of beer, then there's a good chance one of your students is gonna walk by you at that exact moment.

We meet with all of our student teachers as a big group every semester. The first thing we tell them is, "Go right home this afternoon and check your Facebook page. If you wouldn't want your grandmother seeing what's on there, you need to pull it down." This applies not just to photos, but posts where your friends might be cussing or saying inappropriate things. Because the very first thing a parent or a kid's gonna do when they get a new teacher is look at your Facebook and Instagram

WAYS TO SPOT TEACHER FRIENDS
AT THE BEACH

- They got on some of them skirty bathing suits with big old floppy hats and some Lady Gaga sunglasses. They're trying to disguise themselves so the kids won't find them.

- They're dragging around a big old first aid wagon just in case a kid somewhere gets hurt. Even when they're off duty, they can't help it.

- They've drawn a huge circle all around them in the sand with a sign that says, "Do not disturb. No children allowed."

- They blare some Jimmy Buffett in order to not have to listen to any nearby kids, although they will still jump out of the above-mentioned circle just long enough to yell at said kids for playing Red Rover because it's too dangerous. Someone's going to break their arm.

- They've got a little box with them that reads "End of the Week." If a nearby child's Frisbee lands in the circle, one of the ladies will put it in the box and tell the kid that he can get it at the end of the week. He shouldn't have been throwing it near them. But if that kid needs a Band-Aid, the teachers are on it.

pages, so if you've got a photo from spring break where you're chugging a beer, it might cause a parent to question your professionalism and your ability to set an example.

Teachers need to know that there are eyes everywhere nowadays. I have learned that the hard way. I was in Chicago riding the El at 11:30 p.m. one night and somebody messaged me a month later, saying, "I saw you on the subway." What if I had a vodka in my hand, or was cussing up a storm, or picking my nose, and he'd taken a picture and posted it to Instagram?* The world is a small town where everybody knows you these days. When you're at a wedding with your best friends, it's true, you can do whatever you want to with your own life, but when you walk out of that reception at the Marriott and you're sloshed and staggering around, someone may be watching.

It's not fair, I know. I live in Kentucky where we have the Derby and of course major University of Kentucky football and basketball games. Everybody goes to these events, and these are huge parties, like Mardi Gras. Just because you're a teacher, are you not going to have fun with your friends at an appropriate time? Of course you are—but just be aware of your surroundings.

Even at school, sometimes instructors overshare with their students. When I taught in Florida, a parent called to complain because the teacher had told her class that she was sorry for yelling at them, but she was grumpy after being on a diet and eating Jenny Craig. The parent said, "I don't care what she's eating; my child doesn't need to know that." Do your students need to know that you're stressed because you're in the middle of a divorce or having a hard time getting pregnant? Many people can share these types of things in their workplace, but not necessarily educators.

Teachers also get into trouble for their beliefs, from politics to religion to even cigarettes. That may not sound controversial until suddenly a kid's gone home and said, "My teacher said you're stupid if you smoke." Even if a lot of people agree with you, when you bring your own personal opinion into a classroom, it can sometimes backfire on you.

Yet on the other hand, students love to learn about their teachers' lives. Sometimes I'll have my third-grade teacher bring in her

---

*I don't drink or cuss, but the nose-picking thing: very likely.

eighth-grade child to read a book to her students and they love that. Students like to hear from their teachers about their vacation plans, what they got for Christmas, or that their kid's football team won a game. Sharing those personal things, and life celebrations—if chosen wisely—can bond you with your kids.

My rule of thumb is that students love to hear positive details from your life, and if there are any negatives, be general. It's one thing to say about my son, "Jared's having a hard time and I hope things go good for him," but it's oversharing to say, "Jared's failing six classes and I'm mad at him." (For the record, Jared is doing great and just graduated from physician's assistant school and we couldn't be prouder.*) I also think it's better to be safe than sorry when it comes to sharing your strong political beliefs with your classroom and on social media. If you're staunchly loyal of the president (or feel the opposite) and can't help but share that with the world, a parent may question your qualifications as his child's unbiased history teacher.

My wife and I met when we were both teachers at Lockmar Elementary in Palm Bay, Florida, and when we got married, our classroom parents threw us wedding showers at school and brought in gifts and snacks. It was a great opportunity to teach our students about weddings and traditions. Our students even came to the ceremony and took pictures with us.

Not long ago I was speaking in Pittsburgh when a former student came up to say hello. When I introduced her to one of my colleagues, she said, "I was at Mr. Brooks' wedding." And I thought, "Oh my gosh. She's 28 years old." She didn't mention anything instructional or any lesson I taught her. What she brought up was attending Mr. Brooks' wedding as a fourth grader. It clearly meant something to her, but it meant even more to me.

―――――

*Well, that's not really true. He got a job out of state, so I *would* have been prouder if he had stayed five miles from me. Just sayin'.

30

CLIQUES, DRAMA, AND TEMPER TANTRUMS
Parent-Teacher Associations

PTAs are interesting beasts within a school community. You understand the saying, "10 percent of the people doing 90 percent of the work."

Let me back up and say I've been blessed to work with many strong PTAs throughout my career. They've done things like get a gift for every member of the staff for teacher appreciation week or solicit different businesses to donate staff breakfast or lunch for the whole week.

But what's most important in a good PTA is that they know how to work together. I think when you have a positive culture at school, you've got parents who are willing to come support their teachers. Parents, here's my advice on how to make the most of your PTA, regardless of how much time you have to give:

Put your ego aside. Drama might be funny on *Real Housewives*, but nobody in real life, especially not a parent or a teacher, has time for that. The key to a drama-free PTA is understanding when you're dealing with people who aren't exactly like you, yet you are all working for the greater good of the school. You may have to say, "If somebody offends me, I've probably just got a different personality than her. I need to move on and know that we're doing the best for our students." If you're not voted president or you don't head up the bake sale, you're still important if you call up businesses or pick up the cakes. We can't do the fall festival if somebody doesn't run the dunk tank.

Don't stop offering. In many PTAs you get this dynamic of the same eight parents who do everything, so other parents feel like they're not needed because nobody asked them to do anything. That doesn't mean they should stop asking. In a lot of PTAs and parent-teacher organizations, people who aren't given an engraved invitation requesting help get offended and walk away, which creates a vicious cycle with a small group of people doing all the work.

Something is better than nothing. I wouldn't expect one parent from every family to attend every PTA meeting, but you should be aware when there's an event at school that most people put a hand up for, like the fall fundraiser, the end-of-year picnic, or the book fair. We could never pull off the larger events we do without the support of the entire school.

Help even if you can't join. Email your child's teacher once a month: "What can I do for you this week?" He may not reply the first eight times, but the ninth or 10th time he may say "You know, I need help alphabetizing this" or "Can you please color this for the bulletin board?" There may be nothing needed today, but don't stop asking.

Help not just your school but your community. There are many schools where the parents barely help the teachers because it's a low-income school and the parents don't have the funds to send in snacks or the ability to take time away from work. I am proud our parents at Liberty want to help schools that don't have the same parent support. In our Step Up program we pair with a school across the city that has low parent involvement. Our parents provide desserts at their teacher appreciation functions and school supplies at the beginning of the school year. We are very aware of the blessings we have at Liberty and I'm glad to see them shared with others.

Be a PTA dad. Go to any PTA meeting and you mostly see PTA moms. Dads need to step up: they can run the dunk tank, help at a bake sale, volunteer at pickup or dropoff, and take a turn at lunchroom duty. I think we let dads off the hook way too often. People may say, "He's too busy" or "He's the breadwinner," but that doesn't make a difference. There's always something a dad can do. A dad should be involved in his child's life.

I admire so much the schools that do the DOGS program—the Dads of Great Students—where the dads volunteer once a month to come in for an hour. We also have a reading program where we recruit minority fathers to come in so that our students will see great examples of fathers who read to their kids.

Also, teachers need to support the PTA. We have one member from every grade level attend meetings and we strive to have every member show up at least once.

Teachers and parents work separately too often, saying, "You're going to work on my kids over there, and whatever you need, let me know, but otherwise I'm going to stay over here." If every parent volunteered for one hour a month, schools would have no idea what to do, because they would just be overwhelmed with support.

31

PICKUP AND DROP-OFF

An Exercise in Humanity

**Every Car Driver Volunteer,
at Every School, Every Morning**

"Come on, get these cars moving. Hey, hey, where you going? Why are you pulling around the car line? Do you see this big line of cars? Why do you think you can just pull around everybody? You ain't that special, although I know you think you are. Get back in that car rider line. Every single day your kid sees you breaking the school rule. Maybe that's why your kid's breaking school rules every single day. Don't make me come over there."

"Hey, little girl, pick that up. Do you see that? That's right, that thing that just fell out your van. Mama, look, I'm just gonna be honest with you, you've gotta clean this van up. It's every single day we open this van door and out pop some Barbie dolls or some Transformers or some McDonald's french fries. We don't have time to wait in line to put everything back in your van, every day. I'm serious."

"Excuse me, ma'am, why are you brushing your child's hair in the car rider line? Do you see that you're holding up this entire car line? You can't do that. Look, right there's an empty spot. I'm gonna call that 'the beauty parlor spot.' You pull in there every day and you can put as many barrettes in that child's hair as you want to but don't be holding up the car rider line."

"Why are you beeping? Do you think this line is gonna go any faster when you beep? What you mean you gotta get to work? Everybody in this line's gotta get somewhere. How about this, how about you come five minutes early to school, then you won't gotta be beeping everybody, getting on everybody's nerves."

Parents are often at their rudest during pickup and drop-off. I get calls all morning from parents who yell about how slow the car rider line is, how the traffic assistant was rude to a parent who tried to pull out in the middle of the line, or how there wasn't somebody there fast enough to help their kids out of the car. Well, sorry, we cannot open the car door for 400 kids. My staff can look to see if a student needs help pulling some cupcakes or a science fair project out of the car, but we're not always going to catch it.

Most parents have no idea how hard schools work to organize a car rider line to get kids in and out as efficiently and safely as possible. Parents, here are the eight commandments of pickup and drop-off. You should familiarize yourself with these:

Don't brush your children's hair or teeth or get them dressed while you're in the car rider lane. If you're running late and you have to finish getting ready in the car, do it before you pull up to the school. Otherwise you're distracted and slowing everyone down.

Don't scream and yell at your child or my staff because you forgot to make lunch or your child had to run back in the house to get his homework and you're behind schedule. You may be frustrated, but look at the big picture—how much time are you truly losing from your day in this car line? A few minutes? It's not worth all that rage.

Do not text or look at your phone in the car rider line. If you look down and somebody beeps at you, and you pull up quick, you've got a fender bender, or worse. Listen to a book on tape or music, or talk to somebody, or just try this on for size—just sit there and use your imagination the way we used to before smartphones were a thing.

Lay off your horn. You don't know why the car in front of you is delayed—a child might be crying because grandma just left, or he can't get his seat belt unbuckled, or his lunch box opened up and he's trying to get it back together. Beeping just stresses everybody out. Everybody wants to get through the line—you're not the only one. There is staff on hand to nudge people along. Your car horn doesn't do anything except make everybody mad.

Follow the directions. The school has carefully put traffic rules down for a reason. Let your kid out on the wrong side of the car, or swing around when it's not your turn, and at best you set a negative "me first" example for your kids, and at worst a child could get hit and killed. I've seen a lot of near misses in the parking lot.

Be patient during the first month of school. Everybody is figuring out their rhythm and learning their routines. Assume the transportation lines will take twice as long in the autumn. Plan to come at the very beginning or end of the line if you need to move through quickly.

Volunteer once per year to help with car rider duty. You'll understand better why the school has the traffic rules in place that it does. Also, seeing the other side of morning pickup and drop-off will help you understand the stresses car rider volunteers go through (especially in the cold months).

Say "thank you" and smile at the traffic volunteers. Let them know you're grateful to them for keeping your child safe. A drive-by wave can mean a lot to those underappreciated volunteers.

32

SUMMER BREAK

For Some People, Anyway

An End-of-Year Public Service Announcement

The school year is winding down, which means teachers are getting ready to be on their well-deserved summer break. Teachers make up 1 percent of the world's population, which means that 99 percent of the world does not get a summer vacation. And while I do believe you deserve a long break, I am still working, so please be aware of the following things, on behalf of principals and 99 percent of the world's population:

- We don't want a play-by-play on Facebook of what you're grilling tonight.

- We don't want to see a countdown to your vacation, because principal vacation consists of stopping at the Speedway on the way home for two-for-one hot dogs.

- Most importantly, we principals are glad you're having a great summer, but we don't want to see pictures of your feet nowhere. Not at the beach, not at the lake, not at the pool. They are feet. They should be covered up. They are gross, and it don't make a difference how many layers of nail polish you put on them. They're still stinky feet. I don't want to look at them while I'm sitting in the school office, alone, just because everybody else is on summer break. If you feel the need to take a picture of your feet this summer, find somewhere fun to do it, like the Walmart frozen food section or maybe at a Krispy Kreme so you can have a doughnut in the background. But, I reiterate, we don't want to see your feet.

We hope you have a fantastic summer. It's well-deserved. But please remember that some of us are working.

If I had a dollar for every time somebody said, "It must be nice to get paid to not work over the summer," I could buy a lot of hot dogs.

First of all, teachers don't get paid to have a summer vacation. School systems pay teachers for 10 months of work, but it gets spread out over the year, and teachers realize quickly that they need to use that money wisely. Even though summer is technically a time to relax, you'll see a lot of teachers who stress because they got that end-of-year paycheck and thought, "Oh, great, we've got money, let's go out to dinner," but by July 15 realized that the money had started to run out. Teachers joke about eating ramen noodles for the entire month of July until they get an August paycheck, but the fact is that they have to budget wisely, especially if they have kids of their own.

People don't often realize many teachers take summer jobs—tutoring, being a camp counselor, or working at Walmart—to avoid that end-of-year financial crunch. I can always spot a teacher out in the world, so it makes me sad when I see an educator working a second job instead of taking a well-deserved break—although some teachers do like to switch gears and use different skills, be outside, or interact with grownups.

Many people would also be floored by how much time teachers spend over the summer preparing for the school year ahead, going to professional development, and learning new curriculums. People may say, "You've got six weeks straight off," but that's often not the case at all.

If you're a teacher and *do* get to take a break, there's inevitably that part of the summer when you walk into Walmart to pick up some hamburgers and see all the school supplies displayed, even though it's only early July. This is like seeing Christmas decorations before Halloween. It's just upsetting.

Me, personally—I don't mind coming into school over the summer, all jokes aside. I can get more done without anybody in the building, I can wear shorts, and I have a more relaxed relationship with the teachers without the stresses of students and parents.

Summer, of course, can be a difficult time for parents, with its own expenses and logistics. It's hard to find a good medium where your child isn't on a screen for 12 hours, being forced to do math, or getting away to horseback riding camp in 900-degree weather.

Student summer regression in children is real, although parents don't need to overthink it or purchase special summertime workbooks or computer programs for them. All teachers recommend is that you read, read, read to your kids over the summer (or have them sign up for a reading program, if they are older).

I think summer should be relaxing for kids—it was for ours. We were lucky to have three kids who played together, so our summers were all about the park, the pool, and the backyard. I always had to work, and we didn't send them off to overnight camp, but we still made time for fun, inexpensive activities like swimming, playing in the sprinkler in the backyard, and water balloon fights.

Not every parent can do this, I know. Some parents must work all summer and can't do much, aside from drop a kid off at daycare all day long. If that's you, I hope you can make room for high-quality time on the weekends, because kids deserve a fun and relaxing summer, just like teachers. Except for those teachers who send me pictures of their feet. You wouldn't believe how much it happens.

PART 9

EXTRA CREDIT
Lessons for Life and School

33

DISMISSAL

Final Thoughts from the Principal

Have you, as a teacher, ever run into one of your students at the store? It's like they ran into Santa Claus. It's amazing to them to see a teacher out in the wild.

Thanks to the response I've gotten to my YouTube videos, I'm blessed to run into teachers now everywhere I go. Teachers working at Walmart recognize me and say hello to me all the time. My family and I were in Dollywood and one of the character ladies came up to me and said, "Oh, I know you," because that was her summer job. It was funny that the park character was getting a picture with me rather than me getting a picture with her.

"It must be so fun to teach at Liberty Elementary," is something I hear a lot from people who watch my videos. I'm going to print shirts for my staff that read, "He's not as funny as you think he is." I had four of my teachers with me at a recent teachers' convention, and somebody asked one of them what I'm like to work with. She said, "Well, there's good and bad," and that's the perfect answer. We have great climate and culture at my school 80 percent of the time. There are, of course, times when people are mad at me and they're mad at their teammates. I think we have a better school than most, but there are probably a whole lot of schools that are better than us.

We absolutely do have fun at my school, but it takes a lot of work. The Gerry Brooks "Purnciple" you see on YouTube is a character. It's easy to be funny every two weeks. I can't imagine being that way all the time. Making the videos is fun, but the key is that it comes after instruction and after working with teachers, parents, and students. We don't run down the hallways doing cartwheels and giving balloons out to everybody. We're an everyday school where the staff feels supported by the administration and the parents and we all want what's best for the children. We teachers and administrators may roll our eyes over the nonsense we deal with from students and their parents, but deep down, we love our jobs.

Somebody asked me how many students veteran teachers actually remember. I don't know about other teachers, but after 25 years, truth be told, I don't remember everybody's name. This bothers me because it would be fun to look them up on Facebook and see what they're up to. But I remember specific situations with kids.

I remember a little girl named Viona from my very first year teaching. She wanted to be called Frog. She refused to answer to anything other than Frog, so we called her Frog all year.

I remember a little boy named Kevin, who came from an abusive home. We found out it was his birthday, and, in a panicked rush, the family resource center lady and I went out and bought him cupcakes, and he was so excited about that.

I remember a little boy from New York who moved down to Kentucky. We were doing trivia and I asked, "What famous lady in New York has a four-foot nose?" He raised his hand in excitement. The answer, of course, is the Statue of Liberty, but he said "Miss Smith, who used to live next to me."

There are those times teachers remember when they've affected a kid, or a kid has affected them. You may not always remember their names, but you will always remember those moments with those kids.

GLOSSARY

Berhavioral management: Making kids stop and think, "Am I doing something wrong?" with well-practiced teacher body language like the "quick change," where you talk normally to the kids but then randomly shoot them a stern look, just to keep them on their toes.

Berscuit gravy: When you get the kind that comes in packets, you can warm them up in the microwave and put the packets in your socks to keep you warm when you're doing car line duty.

Cursemas: The best time of year at the Goodie Table.

Derlicious: Things like buffalo chicken dip, or my preferred breakfast: Diet Coke and a sausage biscuit.

Durzney: Where Zendaya is from.

Finger eyeballs: When you point to your eyes and then your eyeballs become the fingers; a nonverbal way of getting children to understand, at assembly, that you're watching.

Home Depot: A great place to get teacher appreciation presents like a giant mister so teachers can mist themselves with cool water during three-hour assessments, or a Hide-A-Key they can use to store some emergency chocolate in their classrooms.

Hurr appointment: Often the thing that keeps moms from wanting to pick up their sick kids at school.

Errybody: The people who get the email when people use reply-all.

NMB: Stands for "Not My Baby"—AKA the parent who doesn't believe her child has ever done anything wrong. It's always the teacher's fault, or another student's fault, when her child took something out of the treasure box or said a bad word at the cafeteria.

PCD: "Pinterest Craft Distraction"—for the spouses of teachers. If your teacher spouse is giving you the what-for for doing something dumb, just bring up the PCD. "Look what I found on Pinterest! We can make these little bookmarks for Book Week!" Your teacher spouse will get distracted and leave you alone.

The Purnciple: Me.

Surb: The teacher who comes in when your regular teacher had too much Zinfandel the night before.

Urnappropriate language: Like when Billy says, "I don't want no dang fries" in the cafeteria line but he uses the other D word.

Verdeos: The things that are the reason you are reading this book.

ANSWER KEY:
TEACHERS TEACHING TEACHERS

The adventure that I've been on for the past two years has brought many blessings to my life. I've been able to visit so many fantastic schools and meet so many people through conferences and districtwide events. I have enjoyed getting to know some amazing educators whose life lessons shine through their personalities, classrooms, and social media posts. I've developed good friendships with people whom I would never have known had it not been for the events in my life over the past few years.

You've read *my* advice to parents, teachers, and administrators. Now I want to share with you some of what I've heard through my travels and interactions with viewers. I've reached out to the most inspiring educators I know and asked them to share their tips on how to improve classroom instruction, relationships with your students' parents, and overall climate and culture at your school.

I hope this input inspires you as you go out in the world and do the important work you do, whether you're a parent, teacher, administrator, or paraprofessional. No matter how old we are, we always have something new to learn.

Five Ways You Can Be the Best Educator You Set Out to Be

1. **Be a reflective educator.** Take time each day to write, talk, or think about what you did well, where you're going, and how you can improve.

2. **Be a connected educator.** We live in an age where we have access to knowledge far beyond our own. Tap into it!

3. **Be a collaborative educator.** Teaching is hard. We can't do it on our own. Find a tribe and work together.

4. **Be a continuously learning educator.** Teaching is an art. We only get better with time. Seek out ways to hone and improve your craft.

5. **Be awesome!** Always remember that every day is a new opportunity for you and your kids to be awesome.

—Steven W. Anderson, digital learning and relationship evangelist, North Carolina; Twitter: @web20classroom; website: www.web20classroom.org

Five Tips I Wish They Had Taught Me in College

★ **Write down #allthethings.** Neuroscientists have found that you are more likely to get things done (for example, accomplishing a goal such as making it to that meeting after school on time) if you write things down. That's one of the biggest reasons that I use and created the Berteau & Co. teacher planner.

★ **Find a restroom bestie.** I didn't realize until I was in the classroom teaching that using the restroom whenever I needed to was something I had been taking for granted. Become bathroom besties with a teacher neighbor so they can cover both classes if you have an emergency and can't wait.

* **A picture is worth a thousand words.** Students love to see pictures of themselves displayed around the classroom. Try displaying small picture cutouts of each student somewhere in your room, and when that student does something worth celebrating, "carry" that student around with you for the day by pinning their picture cutout to your shirt or placing it in your shirt pocket. They love it!

* **Use the unexpected.** Students notice any little thing that's out of the ordinary. Try using unexpected spaces around your room, such as the ceiling, to display student work or create a fun game using the ceiling tiles as a board game.

* **Join a community.** I didn't realize how life changing it was to be connected to like-minded teachers on a social media platform until a few years ago. It has helped me become more creative and has guided me to try new things in my instruction that my students have loved. Try creating an account on Instagram or Twitter and connect with other teachers. You will not regret it!

—Jose Cortez, owner of Berteau & Co. Find Jose on Instagram and Facebook by searching for @berteauandco and @classroomtopia.

//////////

Five Tips for Meaningful Work

1. **Remember that you're not the captain, you're the boat.** For years, I told students what projects they would do and then I had a thought: W.A.I.T. Why Am I Talking? Why am I deciding everything for their learning? One of the toughest things you can do as an educator is to give students control of their learning, but it's also the most rewarding thing you can do. When I started letting my students create their rubrics with me, I saw a massive shift in my classroom. This opened up so many incredible doors for my students, including building a school in Kenya, collaborating with Fortune 500 companies on robotics, and so many other incredible resources. Your job isn't to steer the ship, it's to keep them feeling safe and supported while they learn to navigate the rough waters that are in front of them.

2. **Fail together.** Kids need to know that they have permission to try new ideas and strategies. The best way to do that is to give kids difficult tasks that they will fail and then have a party. Celebrate the end of each day with a balloon popping "failibration." Kids write their favorite failure of the day on a balloon and gather in a circle to share their failure and pop their balloon. It creates great dialogue and promotes a culture of failing forward. Failure in the pursuit of progress isn't failure at all.

3. **Invite a guest.** Sometimes a special guest can explain something in 10 minutes that you've been trying to explain for two weeks. One of my favorite examples is when we were studying solutions and mixtures and I invited a barista from a local coffee shop instead of a scientist from a local college. It was then that my students made real-life connections beyond the laboratory. Find dynamic people who love kids and great things will happen in your classroom.

4. **Facilitate global collaborations.** How often do we narrow our students' options to the partner on the left or right of them? What if their partner was in Spain, Brazil, or Kenya? How might this help our learners learn about others and themselves? The great news is that there's an amazing *free* tool for teachers that connects classrooms all over the world in hopes of sparking empathy in all of our learners while creating meaningful learning experiences for our students. It's called Empatico: www.empatico.org. Empatico offers sample lessons, and the best part is that kids do all of the work. It has changed the way my students see others and how they interact with one another.

5. **Empower learners.** I learned to use the power of students and their desire to learn to my advantage very early in my career. It's a lot more impressive for a student to pitch a collaboration to your district, a local business, or even your building administrator than for you to do so. We all want the stuff, but why? What is your "why"? When a student can articulate their why, you will find more success. Your community wants to support its future

workforce, and the best way to encourage involvement is to empower your students to seek opportunities for their learning.

—Eric Crouch, fifth-grade teacher, Columbus, Georgia.
Twitter: @ericcrouch; Instagram: @adventureswithmrc

////////////

Five Tips to Successful Flexible Seating Implementation

★ **Flexible seating does not work without meaningful relationships in place between students and teachers.** All students must feel loved, valued, respected, and worthy for flexible seating to work. This is the true focus of my classroom, and it drives everything that comes after, including flexible seating.

★ **Flexible seating does not mean a lack of structure.** Having unassigned seats means that students will constantly monitor where they learn best in order to be productive and successful in school. Having high expectations, increasing my classroom management and overall awareness, and releasing responsibility to my students have allowed my classroom to have more structure than ever before.

★ **Flexible seating is not about the "stuff," it's about giving kids choices.** You don't have to have ball chairs, motion stools, or bean bags to make it work. Simply give options to students about where they work. This could be as simple as letting them stand, sit at a seat, or work on the floor.

★ **Flexible seating works best when students have time to explore and spend time at each seat before the self-selection process begins.** My students often come to me not knowing where they learn best, because they have always been told where they learn best. In my classroom, this looks like Ten Days of Discovery where students spend an entire day working at each seating style.

★ **Flexible seating takes buy-in, responsibility, and ownership by students.** After our Ten Days of Discovery, students create and sign norms they agree to follow to do their best learning. This is very different than traditional teacher-created rules.

BONUS: Flexible seating works in tandem with the engineering design process. Try showing your students the options and space you have and let them research, design, redesign, and create it. Flexible classrooms are constantly in beta mode, so don't be afraid to switch things up when you or your students need to make changes.

—Kayla Delzer, CEO at Top Dog Teaching, Inc. Email: topdogteaching @gmail.com; website: www.topdogteaching.com. Follow Kayla on Facebook, Instagram, and Twitter: @topdogteaching.

//////////

Five Tips for Engaging Young Writers

1. **Display a picture and ask students to write about it.** This writing activity has proven time and again to "up the engagement" in my room. It can be a picture of something fun I did over the weekend, a photo that I took of one of the students a couple of weeks before, or a silly or cute picture of an animal. This is a great exercise to practice adjectives or infer what they see happening in the picture.

2. **Read a picture book to the class and have them draw a picture and write a sentence about what you read.** Children love being read to, and when you capture their attention with an engaging picture book, they will be inspired to write. This exercise also allows the whole class to write on the same topic so it's easy to pull small groups to give them more support.

3. **Attach a craft to the writing assignment.** Art is a lost subject area these days, and whenever I have a chance, I incorporate art into the classroom. Once they are finished with their craft, have them write a couple of sentences describing what they made. It's a simple way to practice descriptive writing.

4. **Provide the students with a "word bank."** Some students get hung up on needing to spell words perfectly and can get overwhelmed. When the whole class is writing on the same topic, provide them with vocabulary words or a word bank to draw from. By providing vocabulary words for them to incorporate into their sentences, you are taking the pressure off of perfect spelling. My end goal is to encourage my students to write the sounds they hear and not worry about spelling words perfectly, but a word bank is a great scaffold before they are independent spellers.

5. **Model the writing first before you have your students complete the writing assignment independently.** I demonstrate a step-by-step example of the assignment before I turn them loose to complete it on their own. While I am modeling how to write a sentence, I show correct spacing and punctuation, we add adjectives, etc. Even though it might be the 50th time we have written a sentence or a small paragraph, I still model my expectations for the assignment before they start working.

—Michelle Griffo, teacher, Southern California, @applesandabcs

Five Things All Students Need to Succeed

★ **A good teacher.** If a principal does his job, he will hire good teachers in the first place. Research shows that a good teacher—that is, one who teaches with urgency—is instructionally intentional; acts excited to be there; and provides rich, engaging lessons in a student-centered classroom in which students can make a year and half's worth of academic growth in one year.

★ **Access to lots of books.** This happens in two ways. The first is by having an "Every day is library day" policy in your school's media center, where students are free to check out books any day of the week, not just on one assigned library day. The second way is to allow students to check out books based not on their level but on their interest. Research shows that when students are free to self-select the books they read, even if it's outside their reading level, they are more engaged and motivated to read them.

★ **Chunks of time to read and chunks of time to write.** Students come to school to learn to read and write. The only way students get into reading and writing is by actually reading and actually writing—not listening to the teacher talk about reading and writing. Kids don't go to swim practice to listen to their swim coach talk about swimming for 45 minutes while they wait to get in the water. Teachers need to keep their mini-lessons mini so we don't rob kids of time to practice reading and writing.

★ **Feedback.** When it comes to getting better at anything, we need feedback. We need to know what we're doing well, and we wneed to know specific ways we can improve. Teachers are good at giving kids behavioral feedback, but often we forget to tell students what they can do to become better readers and writers. Specific, timely, academic feedback is what kids need in order to get better at reading and writing—and this means really knowing your students as readers and writers.

★ **Love.** More than anything, students need love. They need to know they are cared for and valued, and that we believe in them. Teachers can show their love to students by smiling; listening to their stories, suggestions, and ideas; and telling them, "I'm so glad you're at school today!" and "You make a positive difference in this class!" When teachers believe that everyone in the class has the power and permission to be a teacher, students feel their worth is valued and appreciated. In a classroom where everyone is loved, everyone feels a strong sense of community and desire to be there.

—Jen Jones. Website: www.helloliteracy.com; Facebook: /helloliteracy; Instagram: @hellojenjones; Twitter: @hellojenjones

Five Ways to Sustain a Strong Marriage for Educators

Ya'll, we as educators have a lot on our plate. We want to provide memorable and positive experiences for our students, but we also need (and believe it or not, some may even want) to have a personal life with our spouse. As a teaching couple, we are in a unique position. We've not only been in education for quite some time, but we've also taught in the same school for over a decade. This has been a tremendous blessing, but at times has definitely tested our relationship. If you are like us, you are aware of the forever-shifting pendulum that many reference as "balance." You know, that million-dollar question that everyone is seeking to find the answer to: How do you balance it all? The weights of personal life and school life are always shifting on the scale. We by no means have all of the answers and certainly don't live in a world filled with rainbows and butterflies. So, our marriage is far from perfect and far from where we want to be as a team and a couple. But what we do know to be true is that we love and support each other for who we are because at the end of the day we are partners, teammates, and each other's number-one cheerleaders. Here are five things that we practice daily to build our marriage while pursuing our dream to change the world one student at a time.

1. Listen to Each Other

Listening isn't just hearing. You hear that, gentlemen? Ok, ok! And ladies? If you have a spouse, it's important that we remind ourselves how important the other person is to us and if they choose to share what's on their mind, we should handle that conversation as if it's a valuable treasure. It takes a lot effort and energy to actively listen. We have found that the following has helped us tremendously when working to hear each other:

* **Body language.** Never turn your back to your spouse during a conversation. Do not agree or disagree with your head nod unless you actually mean it. Be aware of your facial expressions. Be in the moment by stopping whatever you are doing to give your undivided attention to your spouse.

* **Eye contact.** Make eye contact during the conversation. Be intentional about looking your spouse in the eye during conversations and keep quiet. Remind yourself that the conversation isn't about you in the moment.

★ **Acknowledgment and affirmation.** Tone can help lead to a successful marriage for educators. We have learned it's not what you say, but how you say it. Be aware of how you say "yeah," "uh huh," and "okay." Use full sentences when responding and try to put a name to what's being discussed.

Wade and I have very different personalities. I have no problem sharing all of the 2,394 thoughts going on in my brain at any given second. Wade, on the other hand, internalizes his thoughts before he's ready to share. It took us a while to learn how to effectively listen to each other, especially on those days when we both had a difficult day at school knowing that we would carry our school baggage home whether we wanted to or not. In the beginning, we struggled at learning how to cope and help each other. It took a lot of trial and error (more for Wade than me—I'm just kidding). When I would come home and tell Wade about a lesson that went south or an official observation that didn't turn out the way I had planned, he would always offer me advice on how to fix it on the spot. Wade: point = missed! Ok, I am kidding! Well maybe only a little. If you are like me, then you absolutely know that is the opposite of what I wanted him to do, and I was quick to let him know that I really wasn't seeking advice but rather a hug, a nice dinner, and then a big ol' plate of chocolate chip cookies. If you are my type of human being, that always does the trick.

When Wade would come home and tell me about how the bus duty was stressing him out or how tired he was from the tasks of the day, I would tell him to move on and get it done. Well, I guess now it's appropriate to say, Hope: point = missed! Epic fail if you will. He would completely shut down and shut me out. In the moment, we both believed we were helping each other, but at the end of the day we were just adding extra anxiety and stress to our relationship. It took us a while to understand how to listen and truly hear what the other person needed. It began with striving to understand how our personalities were extremely different and knowing what words to say, how to say them, and at times—many times—how to bite our tongue.

2. Have an Understanding Heart

Anticipating the best in your spouse can lead to a better understanding of points of view, which will enlighten you both to gain perspective. When one of us wants to offer advice or address a concern, we come to the other person with a sense of graciousness in our delivery. When we receive the information, we work on the listening component we discussed earlier. This allows us to communicate effectively and with a common purpose of strengthening our relationship.

* ★ Practice listening to each other and reminding them of your true intentions.

* ★ Don't devalue your partner's concerns or advice.

* ★ Before speaking to your spouse, be sure to reflect and communicate from a good place. We should never want to hurt, seek revenge, or one-up each other.

3. Have Balance

Balancing your education life and your married life can be challenging and downright near impossible. If you are like us, you want to do your best at everything you do. It took us a while to find what that balance looked like for us and how to be consistent with it for the betterment of our marriage.

* ★ Discuss and list your priorities together.

* ★ Create measurable goals in relation to your priorities.

* ★ Hold each other accountable to these priorities.

* ★ Be willing to make sacrifices for each other's personal goals.

Hope and I are very different, but we are alike in many ways. We are both workaholics and want to do the best job we can. Most teachers we meet love to teach and go above and beyond for their students. They do this with the best of intentions, but at times their spouse or families unintentionally take a backseat. It's one of the most challenging aspects as an educator, especially if you *both* are educators. A few years ago Hope and I invested almost 80 percent of our time, money, and efforts into our students. We were killing it in the school building, but we almost killed ourselves in the process. We had lost a sense of who we were as people. Hobbies and priorities that had made us happy all but disappeared. At times we didn't even know who we were, and it seemed as if we were married to complete strangers. It was at this point that we said we had to start saying "no" to certain activities and responsibilities and take a step back. We had many conversations on what was important to us and what needed to happen if we wanted to continue to teach. We decided there is never a perfect balance because *life* will constantly change, and we have to be willing to ride the wave. Upon this realization, we decided to list out what is most important to us as a couple and as individuals. This was one of the easiest conversations we have ever had. It brought us back to who we were as people and reminded us of who we fell in love with in the first place. After we concluded with our priorities we set measurable goals so we could see if we were holding true to these priorities. Doing this simple exercise allowed us to stay committed to our priorities and hold each other accountable for the betterment of our marriage.

4. Serve

Serving each other is one of the best ways we have found to show how much we love each other. Serving each other takes effort and it's a demonstration of selflessness. It can be challenging at times because we work hard and are tired, but isn't our spouse worth our extra time? Serving doesn't have to be something outlandish or take much time. By serving your spouse you can show them that you are listening, you do understand, and they are your priority.

- ★ Be intentional about serving and set a "serve my spouse" goal for the week.

- ★ Volunteer to carry your spouse's bags into the school building or drive them to school one morning.

- ★ Help them grade papers or make a special treat for them while they are grading.

★ Surprise them at school with lunch.

★ Have dinner waiting for them when they arrive home.

★ Help them set their classroom up.

The possibility to serve is endless. The key to serving lies with the first three components we discussed. If you focus on those three categories, you will innately know how to best serve your spouse.

5. Be a Cheerleader

One of the most important components about being married is that you are each other's number one cheerleader. Your spouse should be the most important person to you on the planet and you need to make it known. Shout it from the rooftops. Let the whole world hear! It's important that you uplift them not only in private but in public as well. There shouldn't be anyone else on the planet who has your back like your spouse. Being a cheerleader should be one of the easiest things to do. After all, why wouldn't we want to shout out who we love?

★ Be positive! Always talk about your spouse in a positive light, especially in public.

★ Give him/her shout-outs publicly even if they don't want it.

★ Be positive and complimentary, but don't be braggadocios.

★ Be a soundboard, and when you are a sounding board, don't offer criticism.

—Wade King, director of curriculum and instruction and teacher at the Ron Clark Academy, co-author of *The Wild Card 7: Steps to an Educator's Creative Breakthrough*; Instagram: @_WadeKing; Twitter: @WadeKing7

—Hope King, teacher at the Ron Clark Academy, co-author of *The Wild Card 7: Steps to an Educator's Creative Breakthrough*, co-founder of Get Your Teach On Conference; Instagram, @ElementaryShenanigans; Twitter, @HopeKingTeach

Five Ways to Foster Independent Learning in Your Classroom

1. **Model, model, model.** Modeling your expectations and small details of a task will start the process of creating self-sufficient learners.

2. **Provide engaging activities with student choice.** Changing the activities in your stations or independent tasks is a great way to keep your students engaged, which challenges them to take the lead in their learning. Also, choice is *huge* to help foster independence. Let them choose which activity to work on, which question stem to respond to, where to sit, etc.

3. **Always have instructions and expectations posted.** A simple slide or writing on a board is a perfect way to accomplish this. I always include what my students should be working on, whether it's independent or a graded assignment, what voice level to use, where to put completed assignments, what to work on when they complete the task, and how much time they have to work.

4. **Set your expectations high.** Set your bar high, and they will meet it. Our students can achieve far more than we think they can. They will rise to the challenge!

5. **Learn to let go and watch them soar.** It's so hard for teachers to relinquish control! Once you do, you will see the independence and accountability you have created within your students and classroom environment.

—Ashley Marquez, third-grade teacher in Texas and blog author at Teach Create Motivate: www.teachcreatemotivate.com; Instagram: @teachcreatemotivate; Facebook: facebook.com /teachcreatemotivate

Five Ways to Relinquish Control
in the Classroom

★ **Let students choose their seats in your classroom.** There's almost nowhere in life where you're assigned a seat, so facilitate an environment where students can discover the place that works best for themselves.

★ **Survey students about the effectiveness of your role in their education.** Provide students with opportunities to give you valuable feedback about their learning and how you can better help them meet their goals.

★ **Design your assessments to allow students to create their own paths.** All students learn and engage in their own ways, so incorporate opportunities for them to find authentic ways to show you what they've learned.

★ **Open the lines of communication between students and their parents.** Instead of constantly sending parent emails, phone calls, and newsletters from your perspective as the teacher, integrate ways in which the students communicate the latest news from within the school and your classroom.

★ **Allow students' stories to shine.** As often as possible, take an active interest in their personal backgrounds and allow them to read, write, and tell their stories throughout their time in your class.

—**Mitchel Meighen, teacher at Chicago Public Schools, Twitter: @mr_meighen**

Five Ways to Build
a Campuswide Love of Literacy

1. **Advertise what *you* are reading.** Every adult, especially those who work with children, should be making time to read if we're going to tell kids how important it is to read. Even more, we should be advertising what we're reading. At Webb Elementary we have "What I'm Reading Now" signs outside every classroom, every office, the lunch line, the PE teacher's room, the nurse's station, etc. We want every child to see that it doesn't matter who you are, reading is fun and cool. It's a small and easy thing that could make a huge impact.

2. **Give access to books.** Regardless of what you teach or what your role is in school, we should all be providing access to books for our students. Every classroom should have its own classroom library. We also set up bookshelves in the hallways and have "Little Free Libraries" in front of our school and all over town. You can even watch the Scholastic Book Order forms for those $1 books that go on sale every month and easily get a book for every child in your class!

3. **Provide independent time to read.** As educators, we have to provide that time, daily, in class for students to read independently. Just as you can't get better at a sport without practicing, kids can't get better at reading without being given the time to read. And better yet, read what they want! We should never tell a child that they can't read a certain type of literature because it "isn't on their level" or is a comic book/graphic novel/magazine. Reading is reading!

4. **Book talk!** This one is so easy, yet so few of us make the time to do it. Kids will read what is recommended to them, so as educators we need to talk books—it only takes 30 seconds! Share great stories with your students, daily. At our school we share book talks on the announcements, in recorded videos, through our school Facebook page on Facebook Live, and so many other places. When you excitedly share about a story, it entices the students to check out that book.

5. **Start a book club.** This is one of my favorites. Why? Because we can start a book club not only with our students but also with our colleagues! When you fall in love with a great book you can't help but want to talk about it. So whether that means gathering with colleagues once a week or starting a "book club lunch bunch" once a week, find a way to get together.

—**Todd Nesloney, principal at Webb Elementary, Navasota, Texas, www.toddnesloney.com, White House Champion of Change, 2018 John C. Maxwell Transformational Leadership Top 10 Finalist, NSBA 20 to Watch, CDE Top 40 Innovators in Education; #KidsDeserveIt, #TellYourStory, #SparksInTheDark**

//////////

Five Ways to Build Campus Culture

★ **Celebrate, celebrate, celebrate.** Celebrating and recognizing those around you doesn't even have to cost you a dime. Making time to write a simple note can change the course of someone's day. But don't be afraid to go even further. At Webb Elementary, I make sure to take time to randomly call or write to family members of my staff. I want their families to know the great work that their spouse/child/parent is doing on campus.

★ **Do things outside of school together.** Planning staff outings may take a little work, but they're so worth it. And make it optional. Yes, adults have lives outside of school, so you never want to make these mandatory. Once a month find time to go painting or bowling, grab dinner, or see a movie. Just invite the staff out one night to do something that doesn't have anything to do with school.

★ **Play games.** One thing that I try to bring into every staff meeting is some crazy game. Whether they're playing a life-sized version of Hungry Hungry Hippos, sliding Oreos down their face, licking peanut butter off of glass (yes, we've done it!), or trying to unwrap a frozen T-shirt, we try and have fun. Adults are just big kids, and after a long day of working hard, sometimes we just need to let loose and laugh together.

184   Answer Key: Teachers Teaching Teachers

★ **Be vulnerable, transparent, and tell your story.** Don't be afraid to be vulnerable and transparent in front of your colleagues. Let them hear some of your story. That doesn't mean that every meeting has to revolve around you or should be a sob-fest, but let your colleagues get to know the real you. When you share your story, you allow others to feel less alone if they're going through the same thing.

★ **Eat!** One of my favorite things to do with my campus is eat together. Sometimes I provide the food (donuts and nachos are my two favorite meals to provide) or sometimes it's a potluck. Food brings people together and when you take the time to make something special for others, and give of your own time, people will begin to feel a part of something.

—Todd Nesloney

Five Ways to Promote Art and Creativity in Any Classroom

1. **Create an art area in your classroom that is organized, yet open.** Fill bins with white drawing paper, construction paper, watercolor and acrylic paint, scissors, glue, pom poms, etc., and make the supplies easily accessible to students.

2. **Engage your students with art projects that connect to your curriculum and their personal interests.** Allow "choice" projects that include an option for an art project, such as creating a painting, sculpture, or drawing about the topic.

3. **Interactive notebooks are a fun way to draw and write class notes.** Use sticky notes, foldables, and graphics to illustrate concepts, and give students access to colored pencils or colorful pens to organize information.

4. **Design colorful anchor charts with your students that include images related to the topic.** Use fun fonts and drawings to help students recall information.

5. **Encourage your students to have a positive mindset and atti-tude when it comes to art-making and creating.** Display stu-dent-created artwork in your classroom and boost their confidence by telling them how proud you are of their work.

—Chelsey Odgers, art and technology teacher, New Jersey,
custom clipboard artist on Etsy; Instagram: @hipsterartteacher;
Etsy: etsy.com/shop/hipsterartteacher

////////

Three Ways to Improve
Classroom Community

Class meeting. It's important to find the time to hold student-led meetings in your classroom. These meetings are a short, special time for students to feel heard and appreciated by their peers and teacher. Some teachers choose to hold daily morning meetings, whereas others choose to hold one meeting at the start *or* end of their week. Choose what works best for you and your students. In my own classroom, I like to hold class meetings every Friday afternoon for 20 minutes. Yes, I have to cut out 20 minutes of instruction, but I assure you that it's worth it. The class meeting structure I follow is inspired by the mentor teacher I had during my student teaching experience. Every student in my class receives one sticky note where they will write one of the following: kudos (compliment), concern, question, or suggestion (for the classroom or an activity/lesson). I will also contribute a few kudos to the meeting. I then select two students to lead our meetings. These students were demonstrating leadership and hard work throughout the week. Those two students will read the (anonymous) sticky notes one at a time, and they'll pass out any kudos that were given that week. I keep track of the students who receive compliments, and I ensure that each student is receiving an adequate amount of compliments every few weeks. It's important to note that not every child will receive a kudos every week, and that is okay! The students love this time in our classroom, and the anonymity of it allows them to comfortably address any concerns or questions they have. They also love giving suggestions for activities and lessons, and they love it even more when they see their ideas in action!

Morning message. I started using morning messages in my classroom during my second year of teaching. I found that I wasn't connecting with my students as much as I had with my previous class, and I wanted a way to learn more about them. I wanted to see if they were enjoying school, what their hobbies were, what they looked for in a friend, etc., so I decided to start asking them questions on my whiteboard. I think the first message I put up on my board was "Favorites Friday—What are your three favorite things to do outside of school?" The students came in that morning and answered the question, and we learned some new things about everyone that we didn't know before. I continued the messages throughout the year and quickly found that the students looked forward to responding to the morning message just as much as I enjoyed reading them. Now I incorporate the messages into our morning routine two to three times a week. These morning messages do more than just show me what my students' interests and hobbies are, but they also show me how the students view themselves, how they view our classroom, if they feel accepted, and if I'm making an environment where they feel welcome and cared for. I'll write the message before they arrive, and they'll come in and write their responses during their morning routine. To eliminate crowding, they know that only three students are allowed at the whiteboard at one time. They do not have to write their name under their response if they do not want to, and they know they have to be serious and respectful with what they write and while reading other students' responses. Here are some suggestions for each day of the week:

- ★ **Motivating Monday:** Write a motivating message that will inspire your classmates to have a great day.

- ★ **Teamwork Tuesday:** How will you help our class act as a team today?

- ★ **Wonderful Wednesday:** What makes you wonderful?

★ **Think about it Thursday:** What is your favorite part of your school day? Why?

★ **Five Star Friday:** What qualities does a "five-star student" have?

For more morning message ideas, you can visit #miss5thswhiteboard on Instagram.

Greeting + Goodbye. This last one is simple, yet meaningful. As your students arrive, make sure to greet them (with a smile). Ask them about their night or what they ate for breakfast. Just show them you're excited to have them there with you. Your first interaction with your students will set the tone for the rest of the day. As students are leaving, say "goodbye" to each of them. I have one student (a different student every day) come up to the front of the classroom with me, and we'll make up a quick four- to five-move handshake. The class learns the handshake within that one minute and then we line up to leave. Each student in the line then completes the handshake with the student who made it up and me. It's a great way to end every day, and it ensures that every student feels acknowledged before they head home.

—Brittney Root, teacher, TpT author, and blogger at miss-5th.blogspot.com; fifthmiss@gmail.com

Five Tips for Surviving Your First Year of Teaching

1. **Keep a "feel good" file.** Teaching can be a tough job and it can get the best of us on a hard day. Choose to focus on the positive. Keep little notes, cards, and emails from your parents and kids throughout the years in a file folder. Whenever you have a tough day, pull out your feel good file, look back at all the goodness, and shake off the negativity.

2. **Give yourself grace.** You will not be the Pinterest perfect teacher no matter how hard you try. You will fail at many things during your first year of teaching, and that's okay! Every teacher has been there.

3. **Find a mentor teacher and observe them.** Absorb all their knowledge—they have a wealth of teacher experiences you can learn from.

4. **Communicate with your classroom parents.** You want them on your side! Listen to them, help them, and be positive. Respect them and they will respect you, too.

5. **Remember to take time for yourself.** Teacher burnout is real, especially during your first year when it seems like the workload will never end. Take a step back and take care of yourself. Take a bath, go out with friends, watch a movie, etc. Do something for you!

—Arisbeth Rossi, third-grade teacher, California; find her online @sailingintosecond

Five Ways Teachers Can Keep Positive

★ **Focus on the kids.** Keep your focus and energy on your students and allow their joy to drown out the stress and negativity!

★ **Find one positive in every day.** In every day there is one positive thing that happens, even on the worst days. Each day, find that positive moment and focus on it.

★ **Laugh.** Laugh with your coworkers and laugh with your kids!

★ **Avoid.** Avoid negative people and surround yourself with people who make you laugh and smile.

★ **Use your voice and share your #happyclassrooms moments.** Every day find one positive in your classroom or school and use the hashtag #happyclassrooms to share the amazing things happening in education.

—Greg Smedley-Warren, kindergarten teacher, Nashville, Tennesse; find his website, Facebook, and Instagram at @kindergartensmorgasboard; Twitter, @kindersmorgie

Five Ways to Use Your Passions as Teaching Tools

1. **Discover your passions.** My passion is sewing clothing to tie in to my lessons. Think about your passions and how you can share them with your students.

2. **Bring in your tools of the trade to show your students.** I brought in my sewing machine and showed my students how it works.

3. **Allow them to be a part of the process.** I allowed my students a chance to vote on what dress pattern I would stitch up. They also took part in coloring all over the fabric I stitched into a dress!

4. **Introduce them to your interests.** I love sharing my love of sewing with my students. My fourth graders have loved learning to hand sew their very own pillow.

5. **Grow beyond the walls of your classroom and share your passions with your faculty and staff.** When other teachers heard I had sewing machines, they expressed an interest in learning to sew. We formed an after-school sewing club for just the adults where we stitched dresses for young girls in need.

—Cassie Stephens, 20-year art teacher at Johnson Elementary, Franklin, Tennessee; https://cassiestephens.blogspot.com and Instagram, @cassie_stephenz

Five Ways to Find Balance Juggling Your Professional and Personal Life

★ **Do something for *you*, every single day.** Take time to read a non-professional book, catch up on your favorite show, and take a walk around the block, or head to your favorite workout class. This will help you recharge and put *you* first.

★ **Take your work email off your phone.** Seriously, do it. Nothing can ruin a quality evening at home with your family than getting an irate email. Doing this also ensures that you're present at home and not worrying about school stuff.

★ **Keep the papers at school.** Let's be honest, you know that stack of papers you bring home every weekend never makes it out of your car. Rather than feeling guilty for not getting that grading done, leave it at school.

★ **Make some fun plans.** It's so easy to let teaching take up your entire life because our to-do lists never end. Make time to make some fun plans with your friends or family. It will give you something to look forward to and will remind you that you're human!

★ **Set a timer and GO!** If I could, I'd stay in my class until 9:00 every night because there's so much to do. Instead, set a timer every day and when it goes off, go home. No really, go home!

—Kristen Walker, second-grade teacher, San Diego, California; find her online at @easyteachingtools